nepali aama

• Kathmandu

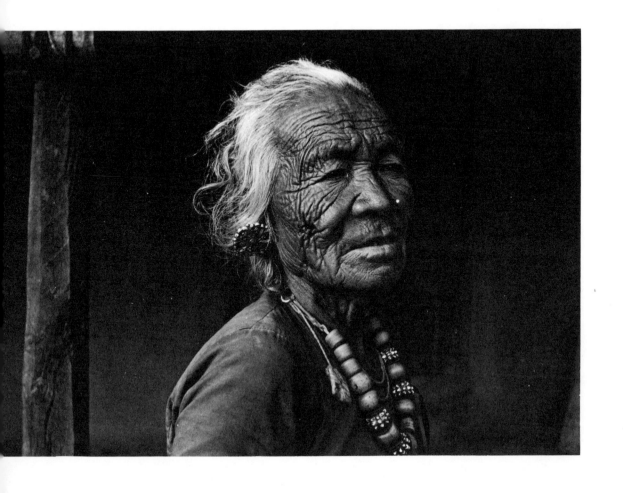

nepali aama

Portrait of a Nepalese Hill Woman

by Broughton Coburn

First Edition.
Copyright ©1982 by Broughton Coburn
Ross-Erikson, Inc., Publishers, 629 State St., Santa Barbara, Calif.
Cover/interior design by Frederick A. Usher & Alma Hecht.
Typesetting by Jim Cook, Santa Barbara, Calif.

Library of Congress Cataloging in Publication Data
Coburn, Broughton, 1951–
    Nepali Aama: portrait of a Nepalese Hill woman.
    1. Nepal—Social life and customs.   2. Gurung, Vishnu Maya.   3. Nepal—
Biography.   I. Title.
DS493.7.062   954.9′6009′94 [B]   81-13853
ISBN 0-915520-45-1   AACR2

Dedicated to the memory of my mother.

Preface

In the fall of 1973 I became the tenant of Vishnu Maya Gurung, an elderly widow of the Gurung tribe of Central Nepal. My room was the open-air loft above her water buffalo, in the village of Danda, a day's walk south of Pokhara in Nepal's middle hills. I had been assigned by His Majesty's Government to teach high school science in a village a half hour's walk from Danda—a walk that took me through two villages of distinct Mongoloid tribes, across terraced fields skirting sharply-angled ridges, and past scattered thatch-roofed dwellings of Hindu-caste Nepalese. A few miles to the north stand the Annapurna and Dhaulagiri ranges of the Himalayas.

Originally I was her unusual lodger, but later Vishnu Maya began to treat me as a surrogate son. She had never given birth to male offspring, a stigma in Hindu society that marks one as being only partially fertile.

Vishnu Maya is known to most Danda villagers as Aama, the Nepali respectful kinship term for mother. She performs all of the household chores herself with a relaxed, quiet decisiveness and singleness of purpose. At first she took no assistance from me, afraid to tarnish my caste-like "master-sah'b"—school teacher—dignity. But with work continually overflowing into the late night, she soon allowed me to carry her lighter loads and execute some of the repetitive, but surprisingly difficult, tasks. Fetching water, churning butter, policing chickens, splitting firewood and feeding the water buffalo were commonly my lot, since my attempts to thatch roofs, weave baskets and plow fields were embarrassing failures. My greatest value to Aama and the Danda villagers seemed to come from the comic diversion I yielded as the butt of good-natured jokes and mimicry. This teasing, however, was preferable to the hopeless unmanageability of the sixty restless and screaming students that were assigned to me.

Each day my respect grew for Aama, her tribespeople and the middle hills of Nepal. Aama and the Gurung were poor and uneducated, but they seemed to possess an uncanny strength grounded in tradition, family, community and self-sufficiency.

I lived with Aama for over a year before taking her photographs. She did not strictly believe, as some villagers do, that photographs will shorten one's life span, but they can be an invasion of privacy. She gave me free license to photograph her, concerned only that I was wasting film on a wrinkled old back-hills lady of no importance.

The following is a sketch of my experiences living, working and travelling with Aama. The quotes are hers, at times interpreted freely to convey the meaning and feeling of her observations, at times more literally to capture the metaphorical lyricism of her perception. Aama's approach to life is unique and personal, yet at the same time representative of other Gurung and Nepali hill folk of her generation. Most of Aama's interpersonal relations concern everyday matters, but her occasional reflections, whether objective, humorous or philosophical, show a profound realization of her specific place in the universe—a universe in which she is only in a physical sense not well-travelled.

Nepali Aama

In the Spring of 1903 in the small village of Simli, a day's walk south of Pokhara, deep in the Himalayan foothills in central Nepal, a high caste Brahmin astrologer was called to the house of Ram and Sita Gurung. A female child had been born to them and it was the task of the pundit to ritually determine the name and future destiny of the child through study of the exact position of the planets at the moment of birth. She was given the name of Vishnu Maya, and the planets inauspiciously showed that she would meet with misfortune and perhaps death at an early age. Horoscopes can change, but Vishnu Maya would reflect later in life that all fate has already been written, and the future course of events are ultimately not hers, or ours, to influence.

On the path from Danda to Simli.

The Village of Danda.

Life in our poor mountains is a great deal of work with little to show for our labors. But even when I have only a fistful of air left to breathe, I'll still be attached to the people and places of my life. The soul always worries and tries to make order from that which doesn't take to being ordered.

No matter where I go, I can't leave home for long. My parents and their parents were born, raised and lived their lives here. Their sweat watered the crops. Sometimes I feel like selling the house, land, buffalo, everything, and travelling around, going where my footsteps lead, laying my head wherever night falls. Since I have no son, who am I to give my inheritance to? My son-in-law's a gambler and a drinker; he was elected headman of Danda, but everyone can see through that. If he'd gotten into the army he wouldn't have had a damn thing to do with village politics. I can't leave the homestead where I've spent my life. Maybe because I know I could never come back once I left.

As time passes, our people have settled more thickly and have needed more food. Until now we have managed, by clearing more forest and intercropping where we had grown only one crop before. We never used to plant millet between the cornstalks—there was plenty of land for each to be grown separately. Now, all the arable forest land has been burned over and plowed up, and everyone is intercropping throughout the year. Some have started to raise corn in the rice paddies before the summer monsoon rains. If there is enough water to irrigate, the paddies can produce two crops of rice in one year. Where can we go, what can we do from here? It seems as if we are working harder, but growing less food. When I first moved up to this village from my natal home in Simli, there were only eight houses in Danda. Now there are eighteen. Everywhere you turn you run into someone. There are more kids now than there are adults; where are they going to live, what are they going to eat? There are just too many people.

One lady in Danda has five kids, and she went to Syangja Bazaar to see about getting some medicine to keep from having so many children. When she found that they were giving out only operations and no medicine, she sure turned around and came home quickly.

Morning ablution: YE ISWAR BHAGWAN KRISHNA BHAGWAN KAI-
LASPATI, BAIGUNDANATH, JAGGANATH, PASUPATINATH, RAMES-
WOR, MUKTINATH...

I can never remember the names of the gods if someone asks me, but
they come to me every night at bedtime and every morning when I wash
my face. In honor of these gods, when the new moon falls on a Monday
we bathe at the well before speaking to anybody.

We have a rule for health. First thing in the morning, even if you don't
have to crap, you should at least go out to the field, squat, take a pull
on a cigarette, fart and come back.

We used to have what we called the *rodi* house—it was a house in the village where all the unmarried boys and girls would go to sing and talk. After the evening meal the girls would come and start the fire and set out the sitting mats. Then the boys would come and start off by smoking tobacco in a large hookah. Then they would warm up the *dampha* drum, to tighten the skin. The other drums didn't need warming. Then we would all sing. Occasionally the boys from our village would go to other villages, and those boys would come to our village for the *rodi*. It was on these evenings that we became shy, and tried to give them a good impression. We all slept there on the floor if we were tired, and in the morning would return to work in the fields or forest.

For two years I was a *ghaanto* dancer. Another girl and I dressed in our best velvet blouses and gold jewelry and silver anklets. To do the *ghaanto* we were blindfolded and then danced in unison, moving just as the other moved. The boys played the drums and flute while the girls sat and sang. We practiced for days before we could dance well enough to perform before the village. If we confused our moves in the middle of a dance, we always knew it because everyone would laugh.

A new grandchild.

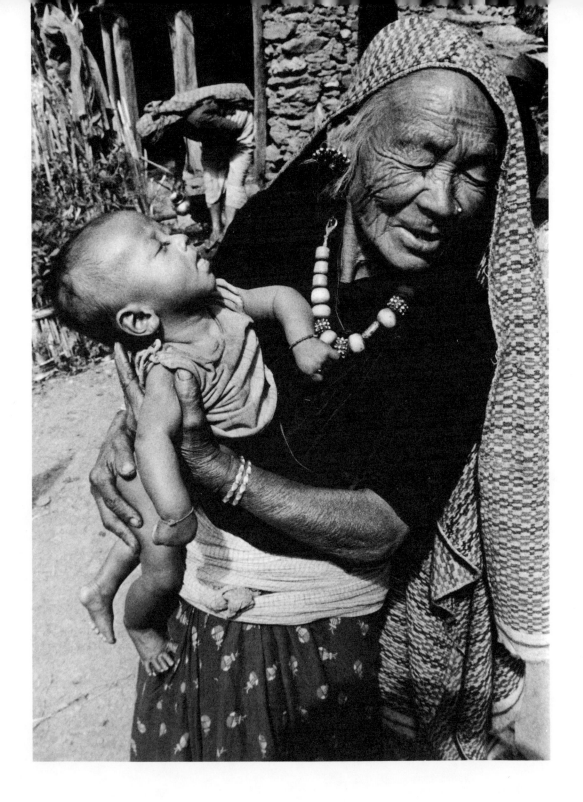

At least one night each year our question and answer songs crisscrossed the village. The unmarried boys would gather on one side and the girls on the other side of Simli. Each party would alternate singing verses of the songs we all knew, and then one boy would lead off with a challenging verse to a girl that he was serious about. He might sing, "If you are so beautiful and clever, then why do I see you spending your days digging in the earth and carrying dung?" All of us would sing the refrain, and then she might answer in rhyme, "With village boys all as ugly and lazy as you to choose from, I would rather carry dung at my parents' home than suffer the burden of your base desires." We would sing the refrain again and he might respond, "You are waiting for a wealthy army man to take you around the world, but where is he? Can you pull him from your goiter when you are an old woman?"

This questioning play would go on until sunrise, and each of them needed sharp wits to match the other. The rest of us coached our boy or girl, and if the girl couldn't respond to all of the boy's parries, she was obliged to marry him. One of my nieces found her husband this way. I think because she gave up trying to match him. But she was more anxious to leave her parents' home than most of us young girls.

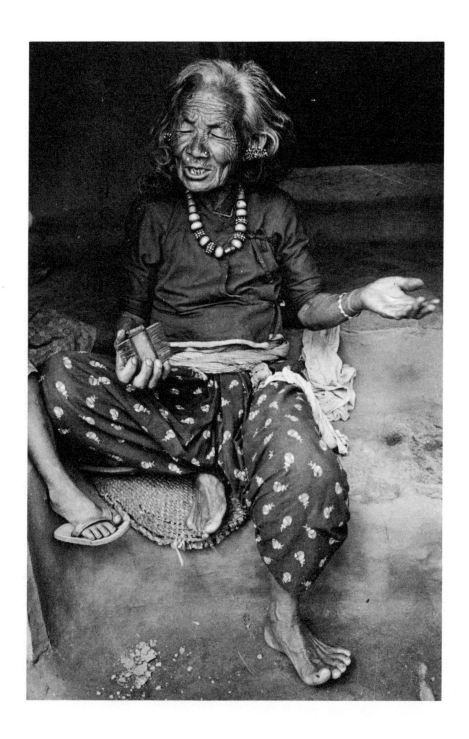

When the parents of a son decide it is time that he get married, they choose a young girl from the village and call a Brahmin astrologer to determine the compatibility of their planets. If the pundit declares them to be compatible, then the parents of the boy send some fried bread and a wooden butter churn to the house of the parents of the girl, leaving it on their doorstep. If the girl's parents eat the bread, empty and rinse the churn and return it, then it means they have consented. Here in the hills, when both the parents and planets pair them, it is difficult to annul the match. The couple may not get married for some time later, but when the churn has been emptied and returned, then the villagers know that the daughter has been spoken for.

Normally a bride isn't told of her forthcoming marriage until the day of the event. One day when our neighborhood work group was weeding in the rice paddies, my friends told me the date of my wedding; they had overheard it in the village. On that day I arose early and went out and hid in the corn fields. When the bridegroom's party arrived and found me missing, they sent people out to look for me. I was fifteen years old. They considered taking my young sister, since it is inauspicious for the bridegroom's party to return to their village without a bride. My sister was only seven or eight years old, and my parents balked because she was so young. Toward afternoon they finally discovered me, and I went through with it, crying the whole time. I felt as if everyone was looking down at me and walking all over me. The only time I've felt that way since was when my daughter's father died, and at the commemorative funeral rite three months later. It would have been easier if my mother was there, but she died when I was eight years old, right after youngest sister was born.

At my husband's home I couldn't even blow my nose when the in-laws were around, and that's just when my nose would run—I was that scared of them. While eating, I was always afraid I might belch or fart. They used to tease me, too—"You've moved only a stone's throw from your natal home; what would you be like if you had moved over the next ridge? Ha, ha, ha." But if a daughter-in-law is forward or assertive, she is thought to be a housebreaker. It is important for one's dharma and the unity of the home that the newly arrived daughter-in-law show respect for her husband and his parents.

On the day I was married, we could hear the groom's wedding party coming from quite a distance, almost from the time they left the village here. My husband, following right behind the band of musicians, wore all white. When they arrived, he touched his forehead to my parents' feet as a sign of respect. We then sat together on the porch, and my parents pressed colored rice, *maaur*, onto our foreheads as blessing. The Brahmin priest then sanctified the marriage. My husband's party and our bridal party both spent the night at our house, singing and dancing and drinking. The next day, the groom's party collected the copper urns our party had given as dowry, called the musicians again and gathered to return with me to Danda. The groom's party stopped along the trail, halfway between the villages, to slaughter the goat that was presented to them by our bridal party. They then cooked the goat, rice and fish, and ate it all right there. And they drank more, too.

I was carried to my husband's home by my uncle's *Gaarthi* slaves. The *Gaarthi* are the only caste that can carry brides in the *doli*, a hammock that is suspended from a bamboo pole, with a man at each end. They were orphans of untouchable caste parents and lived in a small house near ours. Their job was to manage the livestock and to wash my uncle's feet each morning. They were freed by law soon after I was married, but at that time they were bought and sold just like water buffalo.

Nowadays for marriages, the bridegroom dresses up in fancy clothes, wears sunglasses and flower garlands, and carries an umbrella and a radio; it's difficult to distinguish the groom from the other men in the wedding party.

Also, young girls now refuse to be married off at an unripe age. They probably want to wait and see which of the village boys will get rich or be accepted into the army.

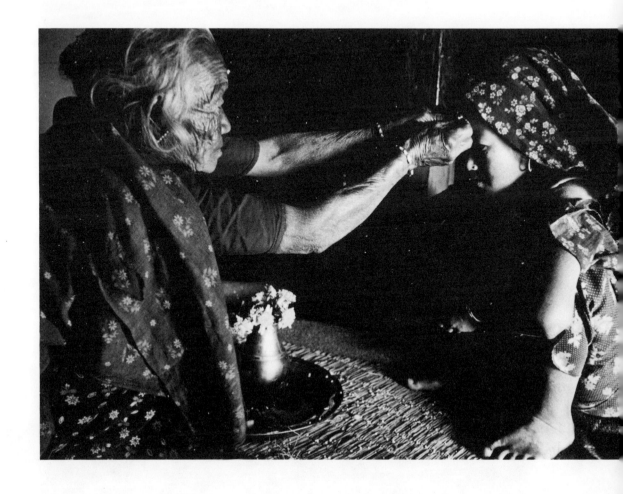

May you marry a wealthy army pensioner, bear many sons
and live to be my age, OM NARAYAN...

You'd never believe that that hillside was all jungle when I was a girl; now it's all buffalos and people.

This land here below the ridge used to be cultivated; my uncles planted millet and corn there. But they felt too much of our pasture land was being dug up to grow crops. Without good pasture we can't raise cattle, and without cattle we wouldn't have milk or the dung to fertilize our fields. So my uncles had a meeting and decided to return the land to pasture. They performed a small ceremony to protect it from further cultivation: they broadcast salt on the terraces. When this is done no descendant for two generations may farm it, unless there is a serious famine. I don't know how we'll survive the two generations without cultivating that land. There used to be all the land we needed right near the village, enough so that everyone could grow rice, beans and vegetables. Now everyone just grows millet, and there's not even enough of that to go around. These terraces of corn and millet that you see here— nobody would have dreamed that they could be anything beside second-class grazing scrub. On the trail from here to Simli, we were afraid to go alone through the jungle that used to be where the fields are now.

If you look at my land, it looks like a lot, but that's only because pieces are scattered in so many places—a terrace here and a terrace there. Just as the branches of families split off—some die, some go into the army, some have disagreements—so do the plots of land become smaller and separated. My fields don't get much water, so the yield is low. Of the corn shoots that do come up, if the hail doesn't get them, the monkeys will.

Change always comes. We own land and we say that it is "our" land, but two and three generations later, who is it that owns our land? In a hundred years none of us will be here. Even the trails of my youth have changed or been moved, and I have seen streams and rivers change their courses.

The trick to weeding crops is to leave enough weed sprouts so they will come up again. We have to make sure that there will always be enough work to do!

We weed the corn first when it reaches the height of our hand. It's important to dig right around the base of the stalks, taking care to chop off some of the roots. In that way the corn plant sends out extra roots from the places where they are cut, and it will grow stronger. Wind is a big problem—it knocks over the taller plants if they haven't grown a mass of strong roots. The corn is weeded again when it is waist-high—by then the roots are fully spread out. This time we must avoid the roots as we dig with the hoe, and pile the loose soil around the base of the stalks to strengthen the plants even more. As soon as the corn weeding is completed, a new season will come and bring its work with it.

We say that we split the crop evenly when we sharecrop, but this is far from what actually happens. The blacksmiths who work our rice paddies don't work as hard as they would if it were their own fields, and they cheat when they divide the crop. They complain all season long about how poorly the rice stand looks, so that we won't feel bad when our share of the harvest looks suspiciously small.

Transplanting millet shoots.

Sifting millet after threshing. When the grains are threshed and stored outside at night, a ring of fire ashes should be drawn around the pile at sunset to ward away evil spirits. We also bury a sickle in the pile, with its blade sticking out the top.

Millet harvest.

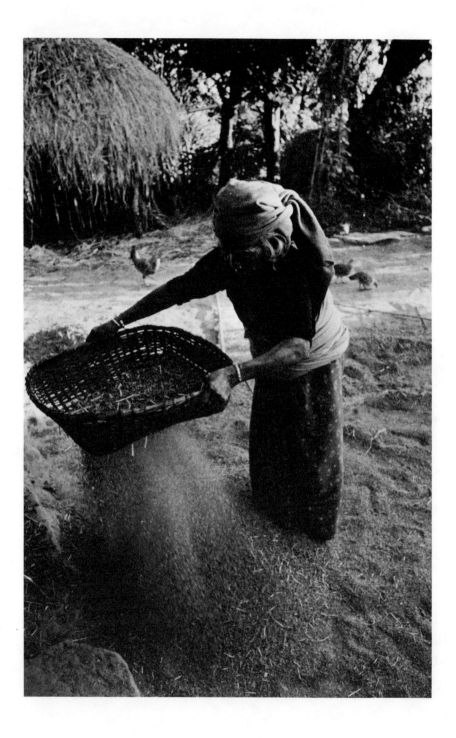

I didn't know what a headache was until I went on my first trip to India, when I was 18 years old. Nowadays even small children complain of headaches.

When we were stationed near Calcutta I was sick for over a year with high fevers and chills—malaria or something. Many times I was so feverish and incoherent they said I was asking to be thrown in the river so that I could cool off once and for all. Everyone was sure I would die, and maybe it would have been better if I had; but the planets were with me, I guess. Who knows? I distinctly remember sitting up in bed in the middle of my fevers—here on this porch—and looking out where all those trees are. I saw the most beautiful rolling pastures, with no weeds, and evenly spaced trees between the terraces. I sat there and told everyone what I was seeing; soon they sent for my nephew, the shaman who lives down the hill. He went into a trance, and my mother and father-in-law sacrificed chickens, and they stayed up most of the night chanting. I was better within a week.

The village lamas used to take people with malaria three-and-a-half day's walk north of here, to a hot spring flowing out of a mountain. If you touch the limey water with your finger or toe you'll get a bad burn, but it's not so bad if you jump straight in, kar-pluck-a. The malaria patients jump in, get out and eat two pounds of goat meat cooked in hot peppers, and then roll up in layers of blankets. The malaria disease is drawn right out through the blankets.

When some people get sick they keep taking more and more medicine, trying different kinds in hopes that one might cure them. They are just throwing their money away, since they are not trying to find the cause of their illness. The cure is to get rid of the cause of the illness.

There's a small bug with an even smaller head that you can sometimes see in fine soil—it is good medicine for toothaches. Pick one out and wrap it in a thin piece of cloth and tie it with a short length of string. Then hang it from the earring hole on the opposite side of your face from the toothache. This should be done only on a Monday or a Tuesday. If you can't find that small red bug, then you can also use a special kind of wire—it's called a telephone wire—and make a loop earring from it and wear it in the same way.

Women will go deaf if they don't have their ears pierced.

My nieces borrowed all the gold I had, deposited it in the bank as collateral for loans, and now they can't pay the loans back. I'll never see the gold again. Its value has doubled in the last five years. Where will I get the extra money I need to live? I can't loan it to myself.

Interest rates for borrowing money have gone up from ten percent a year to ten percent every five months. When you need money, you don't have any choice but to pay.

When we were young girls we wore gold here and here and here, all over our bodies. Our heads were a load to carry around, and everyone knew when we were coming by the tinkling sound it all made. I wore heavy gold discs in my ears which fit loosely near the cheekbone here. I would sit in the sun on a hot day and when I turned to talk to someone, I'd burn myself on the hot jewelry!

In India, the soldiers used to tease us when we wore all of our gold; they'd laugh and say, "That's all just brass; if that were real gold your ears and noses would be stretched out of shape by the weight of all those ornaments." But the Punjabis knew, and they called us "the gold people."

I took off much of my gold after Sun Maya's father died, and it's since been sold or melted down into something else. Where has it all gone? When you can't grow enough food to join your hand to your mouth, you have to start buying rations. In these hard times, who's going to wear all of that gold, even if they had it?

As part of our *dharma*, we used to leave a flame burning in the kitchen firepit all day long on the next to the last day of each month. With firewood as scarce as it is these days, most of us have given up that practice. The forests are disappearing too quickly. We're slowly chipping away at them. The forests get four or five months of rest during the monsoon, but in the fall the tree felling begins again.

One of these clever blacksmiths said if I let him take all of the good structural lumber from one of my trees, he would fell it, split the leftover firewood and carry it back to my house. Well, he felled it and must have split what was left over because all that's left now where the tree was is the stump. At least half of that tree was good only for firewood, but he sure didn't bring many loads of it here. I can't watch the path all day to see what he does with it. As soon as he gets home he can exchange that stuff for fire. It's easier to do the work yourself rather than give the job to someone else. They ask for more after they've taken their due, and complete only half the job anyway.

I can sometimes distinguish the different untouchable castes by their faces; the blacksmiths and cobblers are the darkest, and they talk in a certain way. But it's easiest to tell them by their smell—not that they smell bad, but the potters smell like clay and the goldsmiths smell like the flux they work the gold with. In India, the hair trimmers and street sweepers all have their own smell, too.

This is the last big beam log I'll ever see in our forest. There aren't any trees of this size left now.

When you are churning butter, you have to keep the temperature just right, or the butter won't separate. When the pulling gets harder, it is almost ready, and you must look to see if the butter is forming into a scum on top.

Everybody has his own problems. Big people have big problems and small people have small problems.

My nephew's wife finally left. He sent her back to graze at her parents' house. He had returned from India and found that her habits hadn't improved at all. She was lazy, would argue with her mother-in-law, and small things started disappearing from the neighbors' houses. My nephew was her third husband, and he had to pay 1500 rupees to the village council to get her separated. If she's lucky, she might trick a fourth husband into taking her. My nephew thought he could cure her of her habits. He felt that she too is just a person, and deserves a husband who is forgiving. They put animals in those zoos to protect both the animals and the people, and that is what he had done with her—married her so she wouldn't get herself and others into any more trouble.

You can't always trust close family members, especially brothers. Times are tough now and you hear more and more of one brother running off with another's property or money. An elder brother sends money to his family from India or Malaysia, and it's a race to the post office to pick up the registered letter with the money in it. Whoever gets it first wins the whole sum. What to do? You can't very well throw your son or brother in jail when your family is as close as our people's families are.

All of this can be explained by the fact that we are now in the *Kali Yuga*, the Iron Age. In this age man has begun to eat more meat and dairy products, and supposedly, man will eventually begin to eat human flesh as well. Then, after all the human meat has been eaten and there are no more people left, the *Satyayuga*, the Age of Truth, will begin again.

My mother was fifteen years old when she gave birth to our eldest brother. He died at age four, on his birthday. After that mother didn't have children for nine years, then my eldest sister and two elder brothers were born. Then she had me and the youngest sister.

Our youngest sister was the next to pass away. Tears come to my eyes every time I walk by her burial place. She died over 40 years ago, but I still usually walk around the other way. We had to bury her because she died of smallpox, and they say the disease will spread if you cremate someone who has died of it.

My sister's throat swelled up until she couldn't swallow anything, and she had pox and sores all over her body. To apply medicine we had to cut her blouse off, because it would chafe her so much when we tried to pull it off. Then the disease got into her eyes so she couldn't see. It's contagious, so we fenced off the house to keep people away, unless we knew for sure they had been vaccinated. Then my other sister got it, and we all thought she would go too, but she lived. Then some of the untouchables in the village got it; Gurungs and higher caste people usually can't get it from them, but we can spread it to them.

My heart breaks whenever I remember these things.

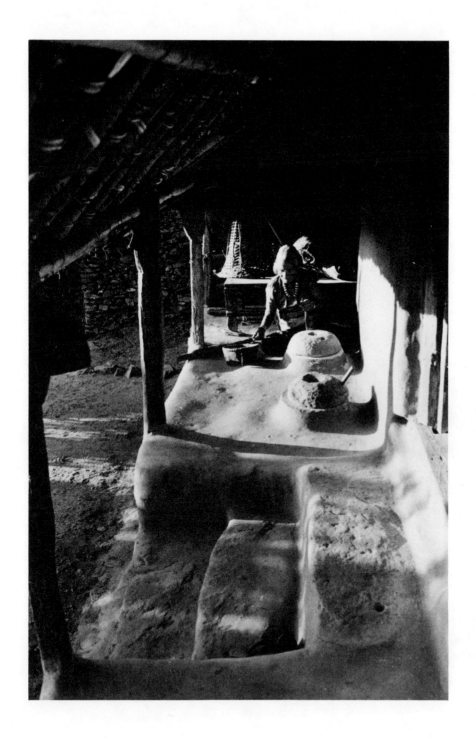

Tears come to my eyes every time I walk by my youngest
sister's burial place.

Then my two elder sisters died. My mother died young, when I was nine years old. People figure that my sisters inherited my mother's life span, but I must have inherited my aunt's life span—she lived a few years past the special ceremony that we do for people who live to the age of 84. Now only my elder brother and I are left. Elder brother keeps saying that he hopes to die before I do, and I keep telling him that when I die I hope he is still here.

It's better to undergo suffering first, and then experience happiness than the other way around—if you start your life and are always carefree and happy, you will probably encounter suffering as you get older.

My cousin's cow was out grazing this morning, so I had to use buffalo dung to mix with the red clay to plaster the floors. Buffalo dung just doesn't have the spiritual power that sacred cow dung has.

Brahmin women have a hard time. They have to get up before sunrise and plaster clay and cow dung around the firepit and all the floors—it makes one's hands numb in cold weather. Before eating they wash their husband's feet and then drink some of that water they washed their feet with. After giving all of the customary respect to their husbands, some are still beaten if they step out of line.

Humans can make a model of a person, a likeness of a person, but they can't make it breathe and speak.

We don't like to talk about it, but 30 years ago a Gurkha Army pensioner from Simli sacrificed a small blacksmith-caste child. Someone—a self-appointed shaman, maybe—told him that if he learned a certain mantra and went into a trance he would be led to the location of a large solid gold figurine. He learned and repeated the mantra and went into a trance, but was not directed to the statuette. Some friends convinced him that if he sacrificed a human, the hiding place would be revealed. At night he kidnapped a baby from the blacksmith village, took it out into a field and sacrificed it just as one would slaughter a goat. He escaped to India, and the police and officials from all over the district interrogated the village. He was gone for months, but returned when he imagined that everyone had forgotten. The police captured him and took him to jail, but I hear that he has again escaped to India. Army pensioners return from travelling around the world, and some of them think they can act as if they are gods. What was he to gain by sacrificing a child? Just a gold statuette and a lot of trouble for us villagers.

The water buffalo is getting old now, and I've got to think of buying a new one, but the trade-in value of an old buffalo isn't too good. She is almost dry, too; sometimes she gives milk and sometimes she doesn't. I was sure she was to give birth when she got so heavy last year, but no issue. When the buffalo dries up, do you think I can get milk from the chickens? The last buffalo I had didn't conceive for two years in a row. She had been with me so long and had given so much milk, she was just like a mother. I couldn't watch when she was sacrificed, and I didn't allow any of her meat into my house.

When I was a young girl, I didn't like to eat meat. I would see it there on the plate, pick it up, look at it, put it down, and then eat something else. People asked me what was wrong, because anyone will eat meat whenever they can get it. I guess I just lost my appetite for it after seeing chickens' heads cut off. Now that I'm old, I have developed an appetite for meat, but I don't have the teeth to chew it. Until six or seven years ago I had quite a few, but now look at my daughter's mouth; not many more in there than there are in mine. I sure like to eat parched corn, but my mouth mill won't grind it anymore—it's worn smooth.

Sure, adults get the biggest shares of milk and meat—that's because we could die any day; kids will have plenty of time to eat their share of milk, butter and meat.

Barely a pint.

There is something you can do so that disease will never touch your livestock. Go up to the cremation ground at night. Grab one of the bamboo sticks that are used to hold the logs of the funeral pyre. Then, without looking back, run home and put it into the gate that the livestock use. You'll have very few problems with your livestock after that, but who is not afraid to go to the cremation ground at night?

Feeding the water buffalo.

Look at this scarred up firewood—last year's big hailstorm
ripped the bark right off the tree branches.

The hail strikes us more in the hills maybe because we are not as knowledgeable in the ways of the gods. In Kathmandu, there are many pundits and high lamas—they must have control over the hail since they don't get as much of it there.

They don't do it anymore, but shamans would go up to the ridge here above the village in spring, to conduct the hail protection ritual. They first wove screens from strips of bamboo and tied them together into big open baskets. Then they would chant mantras and dance for hours, rerouting the hail into the ridge-top baskets. The neighboring Brahmin villagers didn't believe that our shamans actually could collect hail in those baskets. They complained that the shamans simply shifted all the hail and rain to their area and their crops were ruined instead.

If the lamas succeed at diverting the hail to another place, they are tipped with gold jewelry.

After every villager's corn is planted, we have one day of rest. No one is allowed to turn the soil or grind flour or forge tools or sew clothes on that day. We do this in the name of hail, to create peace with the gods that bring it.

We've always had trouble with hail. Eight years ago all of the corn and most of the fruit trees were wiped out—total destruction. But we were out the next day plowing the stubble under and replanting.

This year, there was no rain after the corn planting, so the corn couldn't germinate. If it doesn't sprout soon after planting, we have to worry about the bugs getting to it. Finally it rained and the corn came up, but by then it could barely compete with the weeds. Then the hail came, turning the countryside white and making tatters of the crops. It was too late in the spring to replant, so what could we do? We have the same trouble with hail on the rice before it becomes established. It never used to hail so hard, though, in the old days. Now we get hailstorms the size of your fist that kill livestock and rip the leaves and bark from the trees. There's a crazy guy in Kalku who used to be sane, just like us. He was hit on the head by a hailstone, and he's never been the same since. If it hails on your wedding day, the entire marriage is called off.

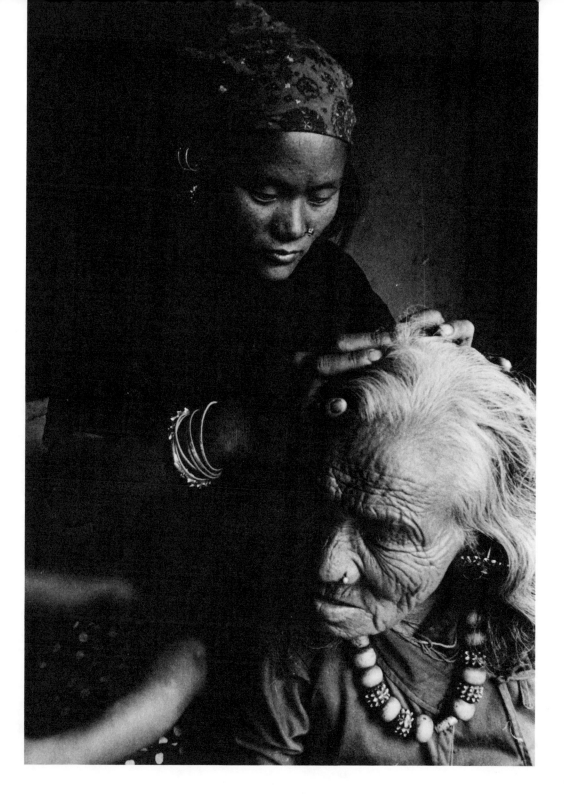

When we cut our hair we gather it, wad it into a ball, spit on it and throw it into the nettle bushes. If the hair is blown by the wind, part of one's soul will fly away with it. If a witch found it she could cast a hex on it. We say that two people who cut their hair in the same place will be bothered with each other's troubles.

The best way to get rid of head lice is to snatch some big buffalo lice from the water buffalo and put them in your hair. They eat the hair lice right away, and these buffalo lice are big enough that you don't have to squint so much to see them, and you can pick them out easily. When you get old and your hair turns white, your lice turn white, too.

My father used to store his wad of chewing tobacco behind his ear. He said it always stayed fresh there, and also kept the lice away.

The search for lice.

Resuscitating an ailing chicken by restoring its lost breath through the other end.

I keep all of the chickens locked in the house at night. Jackals were stealing them from the chicken house, even though it's made of stone and was tightly locked. They can still find their way in, somehow. One jackal pushed aside that big stone on the roof of the chicken shed—the thing must weight more than a man. The chickens aren't safe even in the house. One night I'd gone to see a ritual performed at my cousin's house, and it was late when I returned. I stumbled onto the porch and sensed that something had happened here at the house. I opened the door, and all nine chickens—big hens, cocks, chicks and all—were scattered all over with blood and feathers everywhere, the guts hanging out of some of them. Only one was missing, but the rest of the mess was too disgusting to cut up and cook. That's the yellow-throated marten. It kills everything but it takes only one or two. He got in through that hole in the attic window where the cat comes and goes. He must have finished off the sugar before he went on to the chickens—the lid was off and you could see his claw marks in the jar.

I've been getting up earlier these days because of that old rooster we have. The older they get, the earlier in the morning they go *ku-kaREE-kwaa*. Never buy a cock that crows in the evening. Its seed will be bad and its meat tough.

My best layer's comb is leaning over to the side. That usually means that she is done laying for a while.

I thought this hen was a big fat one, but without the feathers she's all skin.

If you find a termite nest, you can feed it to the chickens. They will eat all the termites and will lay more eggs.

For a chicken that has a bad foot, crush a jungle spider in some ghee and rub it in well.

Animals and humans are really of the same blood, the same substance. If someone comes to harm you, you naturally try to protect yourself, don't you? Small animals and insects do the same thing. Their habit is to protect themselves if you go to touch them. They must be of the same substance that we are.

They say my father was very generous and honest. He was devoutly religious, too. He used to read to us children from Hindu mythology and recite tales of what the people and gods of the old days were like.

One day my daughter Sun Maya, her father and I were walking on the trail to Simli, on our way to visit my parents. Sun Maya's father stepped off the trail to look for a walking stick. He spied a tree in the woods that was completely white from the ground to as high as he could reach—it was covered with mushrooms. We picked two big loads and arrived at my parents' house with one of the biggest homecoming gifts ever.

Sun Maya's father died with debtors beholden to him. There's no chance that I'll ever be repaid those debts of borrowed land. That's the best way to earn land or money around here, just wait until your creditor dies and your debts are erased. But if you die in debt yourself, the path to the final resting place of human souls will be blocked with obstacles.

If any villager came to borrow money, we would loan it to him without question. Now, if you do that you'll never see it again. If our villagers were given unlimited free credit, they would try to swallow an elephant!

The lines of this chicken liver show that we will have good luck. The lines are straight and it is large and well-situated.

When the nectar flow is slack, bees can make honey just by buzzing their wings! They first fly out and gather a starter from some special plants, and put a little bit of it in each of the empty honeycomb cells. Then they group on top of the combs and go *hoonhoonhoonhoonhoon* like an airplane about to take off—you can hear them from across the village. The whole hive trembles like a possessed shaman. In no time the combs are overflowing with bee-juice.

Bees go out grazing for three to four days at a time, spending the nights in tree knotholes and in attics of houses; they even fly as far south as India. It's a fact, my uncle bet a man that some bees they saw grazing in a field near the Indian Army Pension Camp, five days' walk south of here, were from our village. He went over, caught a bee and tied a little red thread around its waist and let it go. Sure enough, back here in the village they saw that very bee with the red thread on its waist, and my uncle collected from the man he bet with.

Our biggest problem is the yellow-throated marten. It's like a cat with a long tail—you can see it on moonlit nights. It shoves beehives off their perches to break them open. Then, if it can't reach the honey with its tongue, it inserts its long tail, sweeps it around and licks off the honey mixed with all the dead bees and live bees. If the bees don't evacuate, it urinates on its tail and paints the inside of the hive with it. The marten's piss smells so bad it makes the bees' eyes water, and they swarm.

Now, all the bees have flown off, and they took their honey with them. Usually they merely go on vacation and come back later, but I don't know about this swarm. They seem like an awful lazy lot—when they don't make enough honey so there's some left over for us. Maybe the king bee died.

When you're working with bees, chew some peppercorns and ginger. Then blow on the combs and they'll move right off and won't sting. Don't hurt the king bee or the whole swarm will fly away.

Aama's twin nieces, Gaure and Parbati. Among Brahmins and
Chhetris, marriages should be arranged between sets of twins.

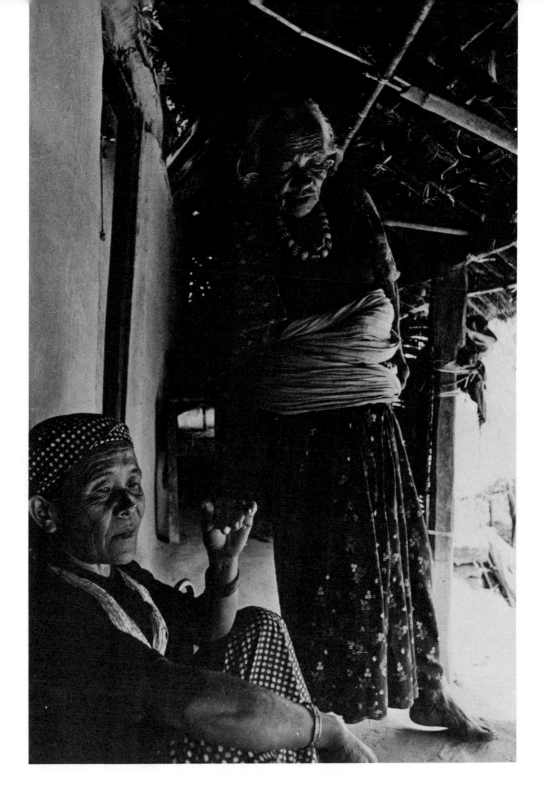

If I were hungry from two days without food, I wouldn't come out and beg for it. But when I was hooked on cigarettes and in the company of people who were smoking, it was torture for me to resist asking for a smoke. My entire palm was yellow from the smoke passing through my hand. They say those new cigarettes with the wad of cotton on the end are good for you if you have a cold.

Do you know why cucumbers are good for people who smoke? Cucumbers help clean out that stuff that collects in the lungs. Once, a man who was a heavy smoker died, and he was cremated in the normal fashion. But when his relatives stirred his ashes they found a big hard black lump, like a piece of coal, where his lungs had been. Fire wouldn't burn it, stones wouldn't break it, and nothing could cut it, so one of the relatives made a knife from it. He used it to cut especially hard things, and the blade remained strong and sharp no matter how much he worked it. One day his daughter asked for the knife to cut open a cucumber she had just picked. Everyone said, "No, you don't need a knife like that to cut open a cucumber," but she took it anyway. When she sliced into it, the knife began to dissolve! So, if you are a cigarette smoker, eating cucumbers will help dissolve the rock-hard lump that forms in your lungs.

I tried some of that marijuana the Brahmins smoke. It made my head go *patatatatatat* and I felt like I was on a festival swing. But there's no intoxicant worse than gambling. My brother has thrown away over 25 thousand rupees gambling. He's not the same man he was.

I can't figure out what today's kids are up to—on the way to school they smoke cigarettes bought with their parents' money and then make playing cards out of the cigarette packs, to throw away more money gambling. They have no scruples about lying to buy alcohol, or stealing fruits and vegetables. What use have we folks who are about to die for these new customs?

The other day my elder cousin Baje was cutting millet straw in one of her fields below the path, when she saw some kids on their way home from school walking along the stone wall above. She scolded them, saying that it damaged the wall to walk on it and they might knock some loose stones down on her. They were laughing and swearing and fighting with each other, and told her that there were some fierce bulls down on the path that might charge them. They had gone further on when my granddaughter Maaita, digging on the terrace below, heard Baje cry, "*Aayuuu*"—one of those kids had thrown a stone the size of your fist and hit her square on the shoulder. If she'd been hit on the back of the neck she wouldn't be with us now.

Kids are such smart-alecs these days. I asked one young schoolkid why he smokes at his age. He looked at me and said, "I'm just the son of a farmer. Farmers have bad habits, and they pass them right along to the next generation!"

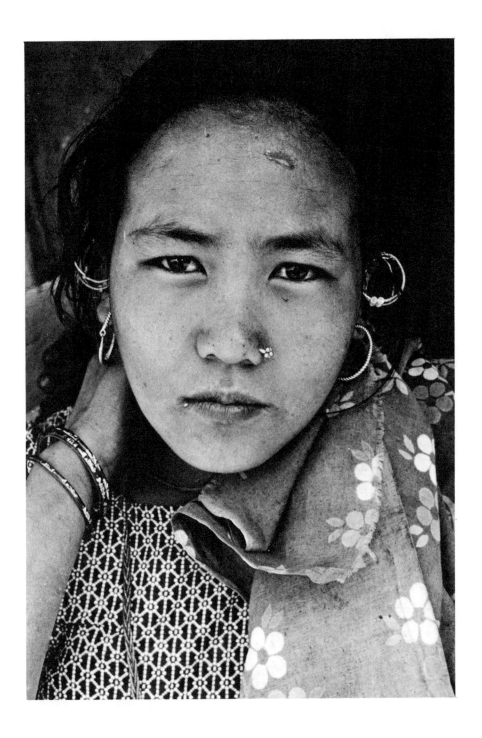

When we were young, we never learned to laugh amongst boys or wear the clothes girls wear now. They like to wear those darkened glasses so that you can't see their eyes. I looked through some once; all of a sudden it looked as if it was going to rain.

With many of the city jobs now, you earn money at someone else's loss, sometimes by unfair means or trickery. Children don't learn this in school, but they study there for ten years, and then lose their appetite for farm work. They move to the city, then learn how to make money. But you can't eat money—who knows if it will be worth anything tomorrow?

People who don't do physical labor probably don't digest their food very well. If you do labor by hand, the blood in your body gets running. People who work in offices don't get that; their brains do the work. Office people have anxieties to deal with, and they have to make decisions that affect many people.

Knowing how to roof a house with slate is out of the question for today's youth. Most of them don't even know how to thatch houses. Everybody wants a tin roof in spite of their being more expensive and lasting only a few years. The old tin was thick and lasted for thirty years, at least on the few houses that had tin. They used to carry it up to the villages in flat sections, a single piece at a time, looking like flocks of little airplanes. We had to leave the trail to let them pass. Now they roll up two or three sheets of the stuff as if they were straw mats.

Saaili, a niece

The nights are getting longer and colder, so I don't go to sleep until the three belt stars of Orion have risen. I usually wake up before they set again. We sometimes say that stars are made during our annual scabies exorcism. We throw some fire coals out into the darkness, and some of them stick in the sky and make stars. There are villages beyond the sky, too.

Granddaughter Maaita writes the alphabet.

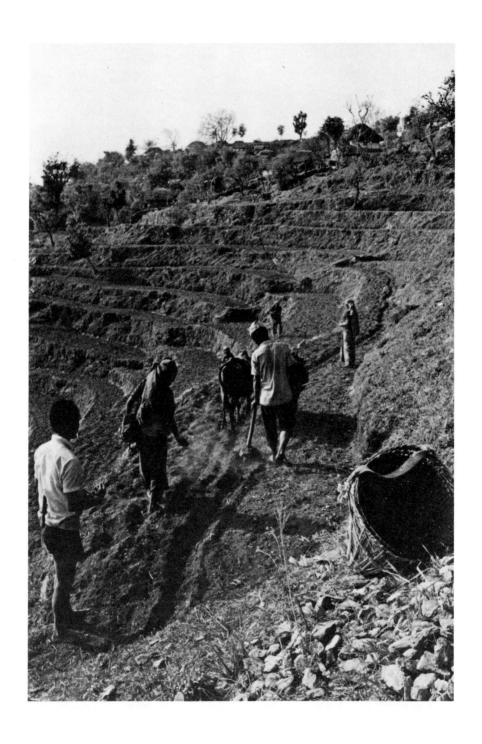

Farmers live a painful life. Water falls from the skies by the hand of god, and we farmers all argue over which way to divert it. There isn't enough for everyone's fields. In the south, toward India, rain water is usually enough to grow rice. They don't need to irrigate as much as we do. But their rice doesn't taste as good as ours; it must be the cold water we have in the hills that makes it so tasty.

If it rains too much, the crops don't give a good yield. If it rains during rice harvest, the rice won't dry and it begins sprouting in the head.

As with irrigation water, it's the same story with teams of oxen. They sit idle most of the year, but when it comes time to hire or borrow a team to plow one's fields, they aren't available.

It is risky to plow and then plant corn in our dry-land fields right after the first spring rain. The corn will sprout, and a dry spell kills the new shoots. Then we have to replant.

Farming is an honest profession. You can't bribe the weather to produce crops. Farming takes hard work and luck that the crop won't be destroyed by hail or pests. Hail and pests are small things, but they have the power to undo all our effort.

Relatives help with the corn planting.

Water taken from the spring will be polluted if we use it before washing our hands and feet in the morning.

The spring below here gets muddy in winter, so I go twice as far to a spring over the ridge to get water. In the summer monsoon season, we can dip the urns in and pull them out full. During the monsoon we had to walk around to the bridge when we wanted to cross the river below here. Now we can walk across the river year-round.

In many places, water is drying up. That is why the wealthier people of our mountain villages hang bronze bells from stone altars above the spring. Once a year, or more often if we can, we dress the shrubs around the springs with sacred thread. This is done to satisfy the *nagas*, or serpent spirits, which control the quality of water, and the quantity of it, too. During our rainless winter months the springs dry up to the point where we must ladle water into the urns. Each winter there seems to be less water. As trees disappear from the forests, water disappears from our springs. We need firewood to cook tea, and we need water to cook tea, but when the forests are gone, we won't have either.

There's a spring an hour from here where—if women drink the water— they'll have multiple births. Twins for sure, but triplets and one case of quadruplets have happened. No one drinks the water there, even though it is the closest source for a nearby village. Not even the men drink it. What would you do if you gave birth to four children all in the same day?

Twenty minutes' walk.

Some women have several stillbirths or children who die soon after birth. If a newborn child finally lives after all of his brothers and sisters have died before him, then we give the child, in name, to a Nepali caste family. This is to ward off the bad luck attached to the child's family. That is why some of our Gurung children are nicknamed "Brahmin" or "tailor" or "blacksmith."

Many women of Danda and Simli have died in childbirth. If the mother is not able to deliver the child, and dies, the baby must be separated from the mother before they are cremated. A villager does the operation after all of us women have left the cremation ground, but in recent years there has been difficulty in finding someone who will perform it. The fetus has a karma that is distinct from its mother's, so if they were cremated together, their pathways would become mixed on the journey to the resting ground of human souls. That's what they say; but a male child will also confer higher karma on the mother than a girl, and the villagers all want to know which it was.

Is it true that Negroes eat human flesh? I hear that black people are that color because of the deposit of cinders and smoke from riding steam railroad trains. Their ears are so big, people say that at night they can use one as a mattress and the other as a quilt.

Sun Maya and the grandchildren come for an afternoon snack.

[78]   If we could eat all of the pebbles that are mixed in with this
rice, I'd be overweight and still have enough left over to sell.

When you wash local village rice you can use the wash water for cooking beans and vegetables—but not the rice that comes from the bazaar—you have to throw away that dirty rinse water.

We never used to sell fruits and vegetables, just divided them between the relatives and neighbors. Now people take them to the bazaar, three hours walk from here. But they don't come back with any money because they spend it all there.

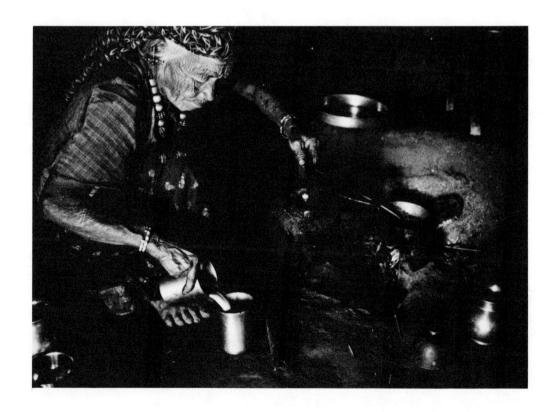

Every morning and evening when I cook, the cat comes in to sit by the fire, and probably to smell the butter. Yet after I take the pot of hot butter off the fire and set it down, the cat runs outside. That's right when I put the lentils in and they make a loud *jhwaang* when they hit the hot butter. The cat must know I am about to do it because it runs off just before I do.

After food has been put on to cook, be careful not to touch the firewood drying rack over the firepit. If there is any *chimal* wood there, a small piece of it might fall into the food. Chimal bark makes you sick; your stomach swells up and you start coughing if you eat even a small bit of it.

After cooking the millet to make mash for alcohol, you have to spread it out on a bamboo mat to cool. At that time when it is cooling never let someone into the house who has just arrived from a steep uphill climb—their smell will spoil the mash for sure.

Teacups made of glass will break in cold weather, unless you boil them when they are new.

No meals are cooked the morning before Desai, our biggest festival of the year. On that morning our deceased ancestors come from the resting place of men's souls and eat the grains right off the stalks, so it would be improper for us also to consume grain.

Once, not long after I was married, I rose in the middle of the night to cook *sarad*, the meal that we must prepare once a year for the deceased relatives; it is at night that they come to eat. Some friends came by and said, "Let's go play on the village swing!"

"Wait, I'll put some rice and beans on to cook, and then come," I said. My friends were impatient. I did want to play, but was afraid to go over later in the dark.

They said, "We'll just play for a short while, and then you can come back and cook the *sarad*."

We played and played and played, and by the time I returned home the sun was rising, too late to cook the *sarad*. I fell asleep and in my dreams I saw my dead father-in-law. He scolded me for neglecting him and his deceased brethren.

What tastes better, hunger or fullness? Anything tastes good when you are hungry, but when you are full even the best of foods is unappealing.

Meat for an evening meal.

Some ladies in Danda wear shoes—not around the house and yard, but when they go to the bazaar or off to the forest. But they all have sons in the army who are colonels or lieutenants. We who don't have a pension or army pay coming in would be pretentious if we wore shoes. Villagers would look at me as if to say, "Oh, so you think you have a son in the army, ha, ha, ha." On frosty mornings it's hard on the feet because that's when they start to crack and split. The dry weather doesn't help, either. Those cement floors in cities are especially rough on barefoot people.

Our money is getting smaller and smaller. But in spite of inflating costs, women have to wear expensive fabrics and the latest jewelry to be selected for marriage. Many wear wrist watches, but do you think any of them can tell the time?

Before there were watches, we used to tell time through an internal timepiece. We always knew exactly when to meet for work in the fields or forest. Now that there are watches to tell us the time, everyone's internal timepieces have fallen into disrepair.

Bands of robbers have come through here recently. They come in groups of twenty or twenty-five with guns and weapons. In Simli, a band of thugs tied a British Army pensioner and his wife to a chair and rubbed hot peppers in their eyes. They threw blankets over the man and his wife, so there's no chance of identifying them, and they took more than thirty expensive saris like the ones the pensioners bring back with them from the service to sell to villagers. Copper and brass kitchen utensils and all of their jewelry also disappeared. They didn't leave anything of value. People value their lives more than their possessions, so when they are asked where their money and jewelry are hidden, they have to tell or risk certain death.

One house in Simli got a letter informing them of an impending robbery, apparently written by the band of robbers themselves. They robbed the house on that day just as they had written. They were cocky to do something like that, but what could anyone do when they come in such numbers? Even the police are frightened of them, and they'd be risking their lives if they tried to deal with armed bandits like these. With the salary the police get, it's easier for them to take a bribe and look the other way. But there is a reward or promotion if they arrest proven criminals, so they sometimes catch them one by one. Two policemen who had come from the district center to chase a band of hoodlums found a notebook on one suspect listing, like a roll call, the names of over a hundred members of their gang. The leaders and masterminds had come from India, but two of the gang were recent Seti high school graduates; most of them are educated. These are our sons, educated and unemployed, turning on their own villagers.

If the buffalo could climb trees, I wouldn't have to do this.

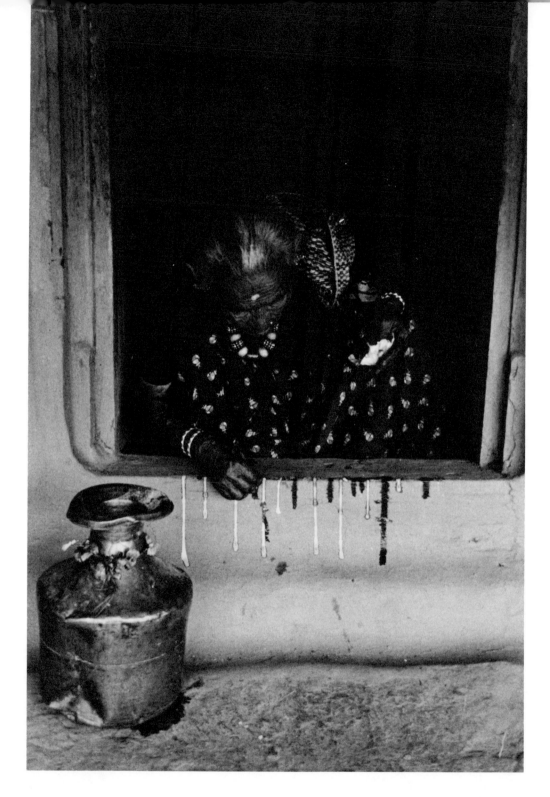

In Kashmir they make electricity from lightning. Water attracts lightning, and they store water in large jugs that are set in an open area. The lightning strikes them and they somehow collect the electricity from it.

The lightning that comes with the storms these days is especially frightening. It goes CHARAKKA and you can feel its vibrations. When lightning struck the house above here, the chickens dove right over the wall that separates our houses.

The sky sends down all sorts of things in its lightning: fire, axes, hot water, plowshares and big metal balls. The fire burns or singes everything that it touches. Only the protective spirits can extinguish a fire that has been started by lightning—even water or earth won't put it out. The hot water which falls when lightning strikes shrivels tree leaves and can damage vegetation and crops. Sometimes a metal tip from a plowshare comes down and burrows through the ground, splitting rocks and plowing up everything in its path. The axes that the lightning brings split trees apart. My niece in Simli has one of those axes—the lightning left it behind; it's just like our forest axe, but smaller. Tibetan nomads from the north come through there each winter and pay money for them. They grind them into powder and use them for medicine; in fact, anything that has been charred by lightning will make good medicine. If you eat it, the pathway to the resting place of the gods will be cleared— if your death is not by suicide.

Once, lightning struck the tallest house in the village. It skipped off the roof and landed on a big rock—cracked it right open. It then plowed a swath down the hill, went through a hole in a stone wall, and when it came to a cattle shed it burrowed underground and went inside. The buffalo and cows weren't killed, but they were startled and would not give milk for days afterward. It was the gods and the arrangement of the planets that decided to send this lightning down on us, but it was also the gods and planets that saved those livestock.

One morning a little over two years ago, my brother-in-law's granddaughter Indra was studying in the eighth grade classroom at the ridge-top school. School hadn't quite begun. It wasn't raining, but there was some lightning and thunder going on further down the ridge. A lightning bolt came down, far from the storm, and struck the side of the eighth grade classroom, on the bottom floor. Poor Indra was sitting near the window and she was struck and killed outright. The students from Danda told me that the lightning bolt then went along the side of the building, like plow lightning, then along the ground a ways, and up the outside stairs of the school to the verandah on the second floor. It then went into the faculty room where it turned and headed toward the headmaster's office. The science teacher was just then stepping through the doorway into the headmaster's office when the lightning struck him, the same bolt that killed Indra. They say it melted his wristwatch and bracelet right on his wrists, but he was still breathing. They carried him over to a tea shop and tried to revive him with spirits, but he didn't live. Even though the science teacher had come here from the *Terai* (plains) and had no relatives in this area, all the students say he was their favorite, that he was honest, funny and got along well with everyone. Some people said the lightning bolt was intending to strike the headmaster, who has a reputation as a heavy drinker and a scoundrel. The following year, I think on exactly the same date, the headmaster's house was struck by lightning and it burned to the ground.

These are not acts of God? They are. If you have to die, then for your *karma* at least, being struck by lightning is a good way to go.

Grain beer is the best treatment for someone who has been struck by
lightning. You should rub it all over the person's body and, if he is
conscious, have him drink some. There are some people who are deaf
from having the net that is inside their ear broken by the sound of the
lightning. If you are struck and killed by lightning, you will go straight
to the heaven that we call *Baigundanath.* It doesn't matter what was
written in your fate or what your karma dictates, you will go there.

Blessing for a yogini.

Originally, all the relatives who came to the funeral ceremonies were fed buffalo, goat and especially mutton. Now the lamas say that no animals should be sacrificed, for reasons of *dharma*. But the real reason is simply that the sons of the deceased, who employ those lamas, can't bear the expense of treating all the relatives to meat and spirits for two days. In collusion with the lamas, the villagers are the ones who create the ritual protocol.

Ritual exorcism of the ghost of a dead relative.

After death, the direct descendants and their wives forego salt for thirteen days. That's why we don't like to eat salt-free meals—without salt it's as if someone has died.

Many years back there was a villager who killed himself. When someone dies this kind of unnatural death, their spirit will not travel directly to the resting ground of men's souls. It will wander about and bring trouble to relatives until the time at which the person would have died a natural death.

Sometimes people can temporarily lose their soul. I don't know what makes someone lose it, but when it is lost the person either goes crazy or becomes very sick. Since the person is in no condition to find it for himself, lamas are called to look for the lost soul. They read from their texts, bang drums and blow conch shells. Then they fill a brass urn with water and tie a thread around it. The lamas say that they can see the soul wandering around the cremation ground at night—it looks like a butterfly, but is lighted like a firefly. So the lamas go up near the ridge, and they stroll around, casually but methodically. If they chase the lost soul as if they were chasing a chicken, it would only become harder to catch. They have to be tricky. When they finally catch it in the urn, they seal it off and take it back to the village. The sick person is awakened, fed rice and milk, and the thread from the urn is tied around his neck. Then the gathered relatives place their hands on his shoulders and go, "*Shaaaai, shaai, shaai...*" His lost soul is returned and he usually recuperates.

Festivals are approaching, and relatives and villagers will all come for blessing. We cannot face them without enough bread, meat and spirits; it takes a lot of firewood to fry breads and distill alcohol. We have to walk further into the forest every year, climb the trees, cut and bind branches and carry them back to the house. It burns up in a second like a match and we have to do it all over again. Then during the monsoon rains, no amount of pleading will keep the fire going.

In the monsoon you wash clothes and hang them up to dry, and a week later they are still wet and you have to wash them again to get the mildew out. When you're old it's hard to keep up with the work.

All of these pots were thick and heavy when Sun Maya was born, but now they've all worn thin and some have begun leaking. One of my grandmother's copper water urns was reforged into that leaking pot there. I'll have to have some cups and ladles made from it now.

I had one beautiful clay pot that lasted many years. I would dry it in the sun whenever it became saturated with water and lift it carefully to avoid banging it on anything. One day I wasn't feeling well, and my sister Chyaure went to fetch water for me. There was a place along the way to the spring where some vines had grown from each side of the trail and made a knot in the middle. She caught her foot under this, tripped, fell, and that was the end of that pot.

We have a saying: The expense of buying clay pots surpasses the cost of a copper urn. The expense of buying plastic bangles will surpass the cost of a gold bracelet.

The inner metal part of a flashlight battery is soft and good for patching holes in copper and brass pots. What you should do to make your flashlight batteries last a long time is to turn one of them around during the day, and it keeps all the spices from running out.

In the old days, the army pensioners, both British and Indian, used to come up into our hills to enlist the village boys. They brought a stick to measure them with. They gave out money and small favors, and even with that, they had a hard time meeting their quota. Now times have switched. Four or five thousand rupees is an average bribe these days to get oneself into the British Army, and the competition is getting fiercer for the Indian Army too. Gold, large tins of ghee, clothing, money and now even titles to land are passed under the counter to these recruiters. Now the only villagers who can afford to get into the army are those with fathers who were soldiers themselves. They have enough capital from their savings and pensions to pay the way in for the next generation. The only way to get a second glance from a recruiter these days is to fill his mouth and pockets.

Every few years a white sah'b comes through here to recruit kids for the service. I hear that at night the sah'bs climb into and sleep in a big sack filled with dead chicken skins, feathers and all.

When army soldiers brought the first soccer ball up to our village, most of us didn't know what it was. Some pensioners were playing with it on the ridge above here once, and it bounced over an hour's walk down the hill, going through the woods and across terraces. It landed in a farmer's rice paddy.

The farmer picked it up and hiked over to Raaipur to ask a Brahmin pundit which god had brought this object to his field, and what its meaning was for the future of his family and crops.

Army pensioners.

I've been to Calcutta—Dacca's elder brother—twice, once with my daughter's father when he was a colonel in the Indian Army, and once again in 1959 after he died. I waited several months and wrote letters to the pension office asking where his pension was, the pension due to the surviving widow. No answer, so I went down there, but what could I do? I had no friends or contacts; everyone said that I was eligible for a pension, but the office people didn't have time to spend with women. They turned me away for some reason I couldn't understand.

Hare Ram, I come home at night and who can I say I'm tired to, who can I say I'm hungry to?

In the old days one had to go to India to see all these types that come up here now—snake charmers, fakirs and magicians who wear those rubber sandals that go *pitak-pitak* when they walk—even trucks and buses. It's all new to us hill folk. What does it do for us? If you have money you can go see all of it. Several years ago my sister and I went to the district center to see a travelling circus show. They had an elephant that could stand up and balance on its trunk.

We spent an entire day lost in the bazaar looking at all the cloth and jewelry. I brought back two shawls, one for my cousin's wife and the other for someone else...oh yeah, for his other wife. He has two of them.

When we were living near Calcutta, we had to eat chicken on the sly—the Brahmins and Muslims there won't eat chicken, and they would have teased us had they seen us. When I walked around the city looking at the endless shops packed along every street and squeezed in every alley, I would wonder how they could possibly sell so many goods.

If you take those movie pictures, don't bring them up to the village. Some people here have heard that you get dizzy and they can wreck your brain if you see yourself in them.

Once when my eldest uncle on my mother's side returned from the army barracks in India, he brought a music and talking machine. It looked like a stone flour grinder, with the center pin in it and everything, and it rotated when he turned a crank on the side. He put these plate-like things with holes in their middle on it, and as it turned he put this other branch of the machine on the plate. Singing and talking came out of it, and we all thought there was a person inside.

We didn't know what tea was, either. The soldiers brought the first wrapped bundles of tea leaves to the village. It was difficult to believe that those crumpled brown leaves could be good for anything, but now everyone drinks it.

When I was in India, I had a guru. He whispered a mantra in my ear and told me to repeat it over and over during my daily meditation. When we were in the barracks and had nothing else to do, I used to meditate, but now I fall asleep whenever I try.

Frogs get into the kitchen everyday during the monsoon. You'll go blind if you get frog piss in your eyes.

Some of the women in our villages are witches. They learn witchcraft from their mothers, who learned it from their mothers.

A witch can cast a hex on a person just by looking at them sideways, especially when the person is eating or sleeping. Some of the more powerful witches can even put a spell on someone from a distance, without seeing them. You should avoid food prepared by a witch—it will make you sick for sure. If a witch doesn't like someone, she chants a special witch mantra onto a piece of food, and somehow gives it to the person to eat. The shamans are the only ones who know how to reverse this hex, and to do it they must know which mantra it was that the witch used. Sometimes you are obliged to eat a witch's food, for instance if you are doing labor rotation in her fields and she serves the lunch. But any of those hexes will be made ineffective if you pass your feet over the food when she's not looking. It's hard to keep from laughing. But you can't accuse someone of being a witch, unless you are absolutely certain who it is that is causing the trouble. Accusations of witchcraft can easily divide the village into arguments. No one wants to admit that she is a witch.

At night the witch takes an active form called *bir*, different from her everyday appearance. This *bir* has backward feet and there is hair covering her body. Nothing can be done for you if you run into one of these, you'll die for sure. A few of my relatives have.

The *khichkanya* witch can cause sickness, especially in men. She comes late at night, as beautiful as a sparkling light, and seduces them. Sometimes the men die immediately upon seduction, but most often they die after three to six months of chronic sickness. A *khichkanya* is a village woman who has been infected by the ghost of a woman who died in childbirth, and she tends to haunt the house of the deceased woman. One can tell if a woman was a *khichkanya* after she dies: when she is cremated, her liver never burns. When I was young there was one young man in the village who was suffering from sickness contracted from a *khichkanya*. The sickness worsened with each consecutive visit of this nocturnal maiden, though at the time he probably enjoyed the visits. The lamas told him to tie the end of a long piece of string to one of her arms or legs the next time she came. He did that, and the next morning the villagers followed the string for an hour's walk until it ended, four feet underground in a fallow corn field. They found nothing buried there, and the man died within the month. If they had found bones or locks of hair it would mean that the *khichkanya* had left her body, due to the anguish of being pursued. She would have no longer bothered the village men.

Don't sit in the doorway of a house, especially in the evening around sunset. That's the time when the gods require free passage into the house and you must leave them room. It is especially improper to close the doors of the house at sunset or sunrise.

I used to know several Indian languages, but I think I've swallowed them with my rice.

When you get old, it is a strain to climb into the storage loft to get something you want; and then when you get there you can't remember what it was that you went to get. You have to climb back down before you can remember.

Sometimes now when people talk, they say one thing, but I hear something else altogether. It's funny how something will make sense when I hear it, and I'll continue talking, but then the person corrects me. Your ears hear things differently when you get old.

I can feel how much hair I am losing because I have trouble keeping my scarf on my head, and I'm getting so thin my waistband keeps slipping.

There's a woman who lives down the hill here who is over 100 years old. But people today don't live as long, and they don't work as hard as they used to. Years ago, people carried much larger loads...even some young people today can't believe we old people carry the loads we do.

Twisting sacred threads for a ritual.

Pilgrimage to Muktinath

In the spring of 1977 Aama and her 65-year-old sister Chyaure set off on a religious pilgrimage. In two devotion and enchantment-filled days, they toured the Hindu and Buddhist temples of Kathmandu, Nepal's capital. Fervently they rang temple bells, spun prayer wheels and circumambulated shrines, as if in competition with each other to see who could earn the most religious merit. They fed pigeons and scolded monkeys, and temple pundits spoke to them at length on philosophy and religion, pleased to have the attention of village women who were, if briefly, unencumbered with daily affairs. Weary of the newness and hustle of city life, and satisfied that they had paid homage to all of the concerned deities, they departed Kathmandu for the temple of Muktinath.

Muktinath is located at the head of the Kali Gandaki watershed, 12,000 feet high on the dry northern side of the central Himalayas. Aama had brought the name of Muktinath, other holy places of the Indian subcontinent, and deities of the Hindu pantheon to her lips every morning and evening since she could remember. She and Chyaure had long been anxious to make the journey, and were glad to be doing it while they could still walk easily.

On their way, the two shoeless, toothless sisters rambled along from village to village, sunrise to sunset, like teenage girls out from under their parents, exercising full advantage of their time away from home. Unashamed of their naiveté, they collected what they thought were fossils and precious stones along the riverbed, and bathed in a hot spring reserved for men only.

At the spring, after unabashedly draining a rum bottle's contents the night before, Aama filled it with hot source water to take home and broadcast in the garden, in hopes that her own hot water might come forth. As Aama filled her bottle, her sister swam over to the hotter section of the pool and remarked that it was a crazy idea, since the sulphureous water would probably cool before they could reach their village.

Like new neighbors, they chatted with the farmers, porters and other pilgrims along the trail, curious about their customs, farming practices, or simply their reasons for being where they were. All agreed about the hardships of life in the hills, but with a twinkle in their eyes betraying their attachment to their mountain homeland. As if travelling abroad, Aama and Chyaure often stopped to jokingly compare their lifestyles with those of the mountain Thakalis and Tibetan tribes, to savor new foods and to marvel at suspension bridges.

Approaching each narrow or swaying footbridge, they would slow down and stop and rest to see if one or the other might offer to lead across. When Aama led, she disliked the way Chyaure, unable to see where to stop, pulled on the carrying bag which hung behind Aama from her forehead. When the more timid Chyaure led, she usually panicked mid-bridge and would want to turn around and go back. By then, Aama would already be on the the treacherous bridge and be more afraid to turn around than to keep going.

Once they passed each other going in opposite directions on a distinctly one-lane bridge. They agreed that the longer they spent on the bridge the more exposed they were to danger. Consequently, they would try to run across, which

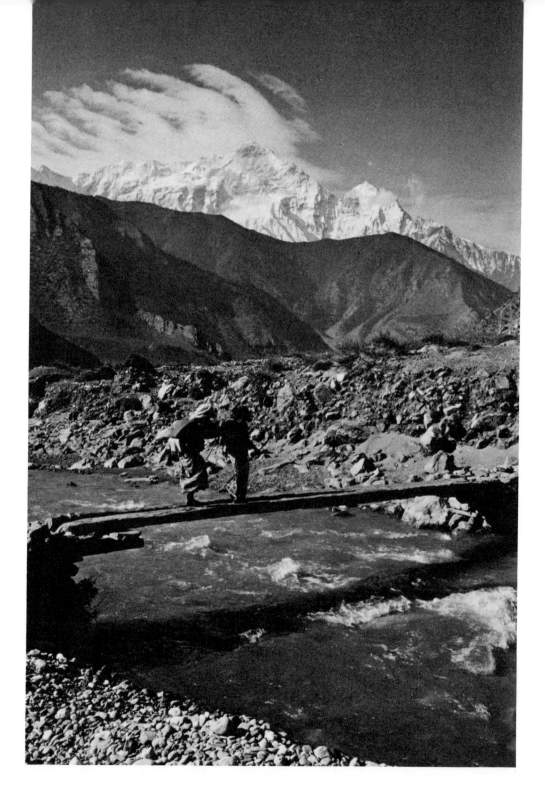

only further jarred and swung the bridge. Hoping to get at least part way across before Chyaure could latch on from behind, Aama continually tried to distract her sister by pointing out trail-side curiosities, but was seldom successful. At one point, however, she convinced her that they were being pursued by evil spirits, and Chyaure stepped off the trail to look for a thorny shrub. Thorny plants placed at the entrance of a bridge will deter ghosts and spirits that attempt to follow. Aama reached the other side before Chyaure found a single spiny shrub.

As they gained altitude, they began to breathe heavily, their pace slowed and they dug deeply into their bags for more cotton clothing from the lowlands. Their feet hurt, but they staunchly maintained their pace, as if immediate relief was waiting for them at their destination.

Many Hindus and Buddhists feel that only through a *darshan,* or holy appearance before the temple gods of Muktinath, can they achieve true spiritual liberation. Upon reaching Muktinath, the two sisters ran under each of the 108 ice-cold water taps three times and made offerings of grain, incense and money to the deities of the main temple. Proceeding to an adjacent shrine, the caretaker led them into its dimly lit, cavernous interior and described and interpreted the colorful Buddhist frescos coating its walls. With awe-struck reverence, Aama and Chyaure pointed to the religious figures they recognized. Impressed that they had come closer to seeing their gods, they huddled at the far end of the temple beneath an offering-encrusted idol. Then the caretaker withdrew a drape, revealing the multi-colored eternal flame dancing on the water of a small stream flowing beneath the temple. This unique phenomenon is considered by Buddhists to be one of Buddha's many manifestations, and they have designated Muktinath the Water-Fire-Earth Shrine.

Leaving the temple grounds, Aama and Chyaure piled

rocks into small cairns as a final act of piety to remind the deities that they had come to Muktinath on pilgrimage. After death, Aama feels, those cairns may expedite her travel to the Muktinath of the heavens.

The following week Aama and Chyaure quickly retraced their steps to Danda, anxious to return to the farmsteads and livestock they had reluctantly left in the charge of relatives. They arrived in Danda nursing aching bones and split callouses. For weeks they regaled their relatives and villagers with Himalayan-sized tales of adventure and danger in the high hills. The successful passage to Muktinath indeed seemed worthy of merit in their future lives.

Bathing under the 108 water spouts at Muktinath.

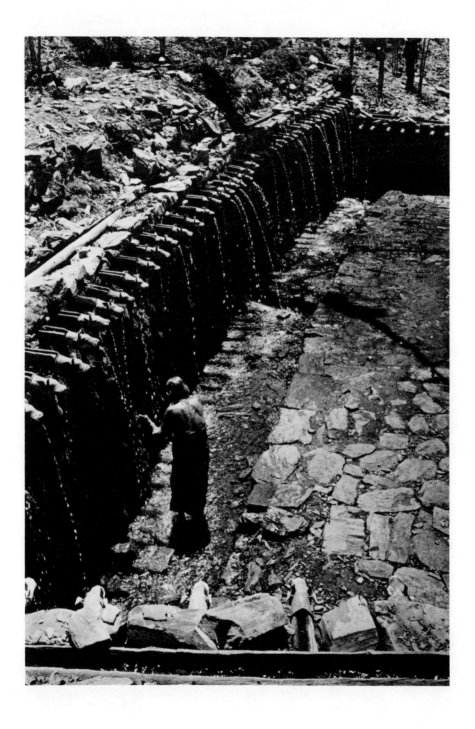

When I go to cities, I pull my shawl down tight around my head to keep my earrings from getting stolen. Some people are very clever—they can steal things with magic.

Brahmins have always flaunted their spiritual superiority. They think their divinations are more accurate and worth more money than they really are. They expect large tips from the rest of us second-class Hindus for their "single-minded religious devotion." But they've abandoned many of their austerities such as abstinence from drinking alcohol and eating chicken. Most of them don't even bathe every morning as they used to. And they think they can retain spiritual aloofness even after they've made themselves just like us. By today's customs, many people feel that if they are rich and powerful, then they have religious merit, too.

Alcoholics are not much different from business people. The more they drink, the more they become hooked on it, so they drink even more. Business people from the bazaar are just like that—the more money they make, the more they want to make. It becomes an addiction with them.

Giving to the poor.

Humans are just like trees: they thrive, grow to full size, bear fruit and then stop growing. Their leaves fall and they die. But new ones grow up in their place.

Women are different from men in the same way that goldsmiths are different from blacksmiths. Goldsmiths are like women—they go *tyap-tyap-tyap* all day long with their tools, while the blacksmiths, like men, mostly lounge around the forge and now and then go *DYAANGK-DYAANGK-DYAANGK* on the hot iron.

Some of the rocks you find along this riverbed can be used to bring rain. The lamas use them in our rain ritual; they rinse the rocks in water, and if they do it correctly, they can bring a rainstorm in the middle of a drought.

In Danda, an eagle landed on the roof of the *subhedaarni's* house, a very inauspicious sign. She had to do a three-day long protection ritual to bring peace to her household; the *lamas* were up each night beating their drums and blowing conch shells.

Crossing the Kali Gandaki.

Boy, bring some of those bananas you are selling. Aama and
her younger sister are pilgrims, and they will need them to
get to Muktinath.

Sometimes when I am traveling a long distance and am tired, a shot of alcohol really gives me a push from behind. Especially at high altitudes, when my breath grows bigger and steam starts popping out through my ears.

OM MANE PADME HUM.

After a mass pilgrimage to a holy place, it always rains solid for a few days. It must be Bhagwan washing away the filth left along the trail by the pilgrims.

When you're riding a bus or airplane you can't really see anything, it all goes by so fast. When they take off, those airplanes look like a big flying rainshield. They give you some leaves to put in your ears so that you don't go deaf. Once after riding in an airplane I didn't eat for two days. All at once everything changed so quickly. When you climb down from one it's hard to walk straight for a while because you feel like you're still riding in it. It reminds me of the time I tried marijuana.

Rest stop.

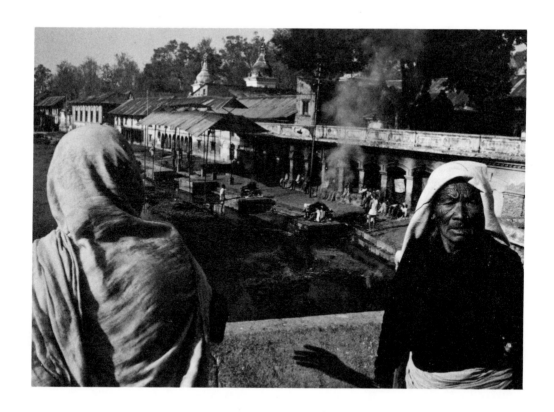

Burning bodies along the Bagmati River, Kathmandu.

It is best for the growth of one's karma to go on pilgrimage to the holy places and pay homage to the gods, but if you can't visit them it's almost as good just to say their names. When you do that, sometimes the gods come to you instead.

Bathing during a solar eclipse is the best way to gain *karma*, religious merit. Six years ago we walked a day and a half to the Kali Gandaki River, which is the same water as the Ganges. It became dark everywhere, and we all bathed.

What kind of offering is it when you beg or borrow incense to burn for the gods? You have to pay for your own incense.

There's a potent medicinal herb in the mountains up here near the rivers of ice called "one pace poison." You can tell if you've found it for sure because no plants at all will grow within a radius of one pace from it. It is good for all kinds of headaches, and can be mixed with other medicines to increase their potency. Only a very small amount of it is used to compound the medicine; a piece the size of your fingernail would be enough to kill you.

Sheep butter is good medicine, too. For ordinary cuts and bruises it speeds healing if you rub in a little bit of it. For scabies, you can smooth some over the scaly area, not so much to keep it spreading further on the body, but to keep it from spreading to other people in the house. As added protection against contagion, they can apply it too.

For chapped lips, rub sheep butter on your navel. Bullfrog meat fried in sheep butter is good for measles.

If you are bitten by a snake, you can extract the venom with a goat's horn. Cut off the very tip of the horn and place the wide end over the bite and suck hard through the hole at the tip. Put some tree pitch over the hole, and if you leave it on all day it will suck out all the bad blood and pus.

The horn of a rhinoceros is the best medicine for ulcers and stomach aches. On a Sunday or Tuesday, grind up a piece of it and throw it on the fire and inhale the smoke like incense. We gave some to the villagers once and they all came back for more.

Therapeutic hot springs.

They say if you work too hard you'll die early and if you sleep too much you'll die early. I do both too much and can't understand why I'm not dead yet.

A clump of bamboo at the edge of one of my fields is drying up, dying. It's not sending up new shoots as it usually does. It must have figured that Aama will be passing away soon and won't be needing it anymore.

It's all written ahead of time by the gods, all that will ever happen.
When I die, I won't tell you.

The Himalayas, The Gurung

Looking north from the village of Danda, the Himalayas—the House of the Snows—present an awesome backdrop whose origin local legend is at a loss to explain. Alpine pastureland girdles twisted glaciers and rock, riding on a sea of clouds which swell from the timberline. To the south of Danda extends ridge after ridge of the middle hills, each one consecutively less angular and a lighter blue, until they dissolve into the Gangetic plain of northern India. Perpetually changing cloud formations distract one's eyes from the steep trails, and alternately give unsteadying sensations of weightlessness and heavy sinking.

Villages of the middle hills cluster like flotsom on a stationary wave. Here, flat land for farming must be seized from a youthful and unpredictable earth, carved from the hillsides into series of terraces often as high as they are wide. Flat land means security, but naturally occuring level terrain is a utopian daydream in a world where every path is a stairway and fields are terraces just wide enough to turn oxen around on. Man and his animals are everywhere. Near villages they have modified the world from the rootzones to treetops to supply their basic needs. Every tree serves a purpose, whether it is for firewood, fodder, lumber or religious respect. Each plot of land is productive, though it may be hardly bigger than the deed which describes it.

Hiking trails, a man's height in depth, worn from decades of barefooted heavy loads and monsoon torrents, meander through villages along walls of stone fused with lichen and moss. The air is alive with the smell of incense and buffalo stables and the sound of chickens and children and ritual chanting. Clumps of bamboo dance to a crowd of cheering millet stalks and capricious myna birds, while the corn plants rustle their leaves in applause.

In central Nepal, each hill village clusters around a common focal point such as a spring. Danda has two springs and they are gathering points for villagers fetching water before morning tea, and bathing after a day of labor. Sparrows, ravens and mynas swing noisily while perched in the bamboo trees around the springs, occasionally feeding on the insects that thrive in the moist soil.

The Gurung of Danda and neighboring Simli are not immune to the mystique that pervades their hilly homeland. Many of them have traveled abroad as mercenary enlistees in the Indian and British Gurkha Armed Forces, but virtually all have returned with a sense of renewed commitment, or resignation, to lives of subsistence farming. All agree that the water is cooler and the breezes crisper in their hills than in the malaria-ridden valleys and plains to the south, and that their "lightweight heart" is a product of their simple lifestyle.

Simli, Aama's natal home, is twenty minutes' walk and nearly 1,000 vertical feet below Danda. The climate is noticeably milder there than in Danda, and hail does not cause as much damage. They are sister villages, and girls from one frequently marry boys from the other.

Raaipur, a few minutes' walk from Danda, is a spreading Brahmin village fringed by some houses of the untouchable cobbler, tailor and blacksmith castes. Each Gurung household in Danda has a specific Brahmin pundit from Raaipur whom they contract to officiate over the exclusively Hindu rituals, especially astrology-casting and protection of the household from infestation by evil spirits. Each house further contracts an untouchable "occupational caste" family to fulfill their sewing, blacksmithing and cobbling needs. A virtue of the Hindu caste system is that almost everyone—except for a small group on the very bottom rung of untouchability—is provided with a lower caste they can feel superior to. Not only do the Gurung have the untouchables to look down upon, but they retain an ongoing economic advantage over the later-settling Brahmins, reinforced by the healthy income and notoriety they have earned in mercenary service. The Gurung's motivation to enlist in foreign service is primarily monetary, combined with a natural desire to see something beside "just hills and corn stalks." The warm openness, peaceful nature and staunch apolitical character of Gurung recruits and pensioners rivals the battlefield bravery for which they are widely famed.

Aama's husband, Lal Prasad, enlisted in the Indian Army. They lived together for fourteen years in Gurkha Army barracks in Calcutta, Darjeeling, and Dacca. There Aama stoically remained as an estranged foreigner in an exotic land, spending the bulk of her time among other Gurkha wives from Nepal. She spoke only Gurung when they went to the Indian subcontinent, and it was there that she learned Nepali, Hindi and absorbed much of other regional languages.

At home, Aama speaks Gurung, a Tibeto–Burman tribal language sounding similar to Tibetan, though they are mutually unintelligible. From one valley to the next and from village to village, the dialect varies enough for her to recognize the native village of strangers met on the trail simply from their accent and inflection. The Gurung that live a day's walk to the northwest of Simli and Danda speak a slightly different dialect. The Danda Gurung acknowledge their barbarisms as in fact the same language, but remark that to them it sounds as if they are all perpetually angry.

Most Gurung are bilingual, speaking fluent Nepali learned from daily contact with the Brahmins, Chhetris and untouchable Hindu castes of neighboring villages. Nepali is also the medium of village politics and the national language taught in the school system. Many Gurung desire to compete for political stature in the larger society dominated by strict Hindus, often at odds with their innate drive to maintain and perpetuate their tribal heritage.

Vishnu Maya Gurung . . . And Aama

Life for Vishnu Maya and other young village girls was rugged but enjoyable. Responsibility was subtly reinforced at an early age less by Vishnu Maya's parents than by her peers through playful one-upsmanship in performing chores. At the age of one, Vishnu Maya was carried everywhere by her four-year-old sister, and at four Vishnu Maya in turn looked after her younger brother. There were few modern hazards to the playful child and her parents were often too preoccupied to watch her. The world was theirs to explore with abandon. They seldom wandered far from Simli, preferring to indulge in their favorite pastime: imitating the speech, dress, song and affectations of the elder boys and girls. In their teens, they spent their days in small communal work parties where song, rice beer and teasing banter passed the daylight hours quickly. Millet planting was interspersed with double entendres; corn weeding was hastened by friendly competition. Trips to the jungle for firewood were made uproarious by slapstick antics. Simple good humor acted as their most effective labor-saving device.

Premarital exploration was, and is, taboo, and privacy a chance circumstance. Consequently, the arts of euphemism and mock gestures are graphically exploited as a release for the social and sexual anxieties that naturally surfaced among Gurung adolescents. Typically, a young girl might demurely flatter a Gurung boy into giving her a cigarette, and then turn around and give it to another friend who had just asked her for one. She might remark that his cigarettes are far too small for her, that cigars taste better.

Aama grew very close to her extended family and the villagers of Simli, most of them relatives, and had little desire to experience or know of the world beyond the nearest ridges. Army stories of travel to India, Singapore, Hong Kong and England were simply stories, made halfway believable only because it was her own kin who would tell them.

Like most adolescent Gurung girls, Vishnu Maya dreaded having to leave her parents' home, but at fifteen she was the victim of a marriage arranged by her parents. Despite early troubles and the shock of moving into a strange household, she came to respect and then love Lal Prasad—"the father of my daughter," as she now refers to him out of deference. It is considered improper for Nepalese hill-women to speak the names of their husbands, and many avoid speaking words that even sound similar to their husband's name.

Aama gave birth to her only daughter, Sun Maya, near Calcutta in 1934, the year of the great earthquake that leveled parts of Kathmandu. Fourteen years later, in 1948, Sun Maya returned with her parents to Danda and adapted easily to the rigors of farm life in the hills, quickly forgetting her Calcutta education and lifestyle. Suitable marriage partners are seldom chosen from the same village due to uncomfortably close kinship ties, but Sun Maya married into a household of seventeen people that was within shouting distance of her parents' home. Her husband was briefly elected headman of Danda, a consolation after not being admitted into the army. He had taken her on after leaving his first wife, who had failed to produce a son.

As long as Sun Maya's mother-in-law is alive, Sun Maya will have secondary status in her husband's household hierarchy, obliged to defer to her husband's mother for daily chore assignments.

Aama's husband died in 1960 after a brief illness during home leave from his sixteenth year in the Indian service. He had completed the requisite number of years of duty for Aama to receive a handsome widow's pension and retain the title, *Subedharni,* or wife of the colonel. A year later Aama travelled to Calcutta on the labyrinthine Indian railroad system in search of the pension due a surviving widow. She was brusquely turned away. Disappointed, she returned to her village by way of Benares, the crematorium and destination of India's most devout Hindu pilgrims.

Benares is located at the auspicious confluence of the Ganges and Jamuna rivers, where it is joined by the mythical Yamuna river which flows up from the earth. Aama bathed here to symbolically cleanse herself of the death pollution, and resolved to forever abandon her smoking habit. Observing a hill custom that applies when a woman becomes a widow, Aama broke her glass bracelets and untied her hair upon return to Danda. After 13 days she tied her hair up again, and will continue to wear her coral and turquoise necklaces until she dies, at which time they will be passed on to Sun Maya, the eldest daughter.

When a Gurung dies, the direct descendants and relatives promptly perform an elaborate set of rituals to prepare the deceased for the journey to the resting place of men's souls, to assure that the deceased's spirit cannot return to haunt the living. The body is briefly placed over the house firepit, carried outside and circumambulated by chanting sons, nephews, and hired shamans or lamas. Arrows are released in the four cardinal directions to ward off evil spirits, and the relatives follow the body single file up to the cremation ground, each with a piece of firewood on his shoulder. Since her husband's death, Aama has had one of her nephews from down the hill carry her contribution; she points to the piece on her woodpile to be taken, and he carefully extracts it without touching any others in order to avoid ritual contamination of the remaining wood. People en route to the cremation ground are considered to carry some of the death-pollution with them, and must not touch anything that may later be used for cooking.

Aama always asks people returning from the funeral grounds whether or not Sun Maya's father's small stone epitaph is still there, and is reassured when they say that it is. To this day, after sacrificing some of the morning's cooked rice to *Agni*, the god of fire, she sets aside a small dish of rice for her husband before serving herself and others, just as she would serve him first were he still alive.

Aama must carry the burden of never having born a son; no daughter can plow the fields, weave baskets or sacrifice animals in the family rituals. She began to worry when Sun Maya gave birth to three daughters consecutively—perhaps her daughter had inherited her own karma. Finally, Sun Maya bore a son. A second son was born, but he died within three months from sickness complicated by malnutrition from premature drying of his mother's milk. In Danda, sorrow is rarely deep over the death of a small child. Sun Maya says that a child's soul is only partially developed until the age of five. At age forty Sun Maya bears marks of the onset of middle age, and prays that her childbearing years are over.

Aama now lives alone in a small but adequate home with her eldest granddaughter, Maaita, which literally means "natal home." (Maaita was named for being born inauspiciously on the porch of Aama's house one day when Sun Maya was dropping off a load of tree-leaf fodder for Aama's water buffalo.) Aama had originally lived in a large round house, built in a circle for more efficient use of space and materials, with a verandah sweeping around half the perimeter. After her husband Lal Prasad's death, Aama found it too large to live in alone and felt the house was cursed with evil spirits. In spite of its ample floor space and spreading porch, she had it torn down and a smaller square house rebuilt on the same site, using many of the same stones and timbers. She still regards the far end of the attic as possessed by potentially harmful spirits that migrated from the earlier structure, and allows only herself to venture there to recover stored grains. She gave one of her water buffalos as payment to the villager who built her house, since the remaining buffalo would supply her granddaughter Maaita, herself, and the cat with more than enough fresh milk for tea and butter. Some of her rice paddy, located in the valley 1500 vertical feet below Simli, was sold as well, and she gave some to her nephew who had several children and could farm it more easily than she. Keeping her land within the family, she feels, will ease the burden of the day when her nephew must divide his minimally productive land among his sons—only to find it is insufficient for all of them.

Aama now sharecrops her meager rice paddy with a family of the untouchable blacksmith caste. The blacksmiths work the fields and carry one-half of the harvested bundles of unthreshed grain and straw from the valley to her house. She threshes the rice by whipping shocks of it upon a flat stone, and drives her son-in-law's oxen over the straw to remove the final few grains. The rice is stored in the attic in its husk, and is dehusked when needed in a foot-operated beam huller before cooking, usually for consumption by guests or on special occasions. Rice is becoming scarce and expensive; most of the land in the middle hills that is suitable for irrigation and rice culture has been pioneered. Steep and unirrigable fields are all that remain to be reclaimed from the shrinking forests. On such marginal land, only millet and corn will grow well.

Aama and Maaita subsist primarily on two daily meals of *dimdo,* millet mush. The unappetizing gruel is made from millet flour ground in a stone quern, mixed with water and stirred over the fire into a thick and tenacious paste. They daub handfuls of it in lentils or fried vegetables and swallow it whole, claiming that it tastes better and digests more slowly than rice and repels hunger longer. Tea and parched corn are their early morning and late afternoon snacks, but since the loss of her teeth Aama must grind the unpopped kernels into flour before she can eat.

About every fortnight Aama "throws her sleep away," and stays up much of the night to boil a large batch of millet in her versatile copper pot. She mixes in yeast chips compounded from a recipe of local plant and animal ingredients, chants a special mantra and seals it in a clay pot. Within a week during warm weather, the cooked grains ferment into sweet and mushy mash. She then distills this mash in the same copper pot, zealously splitting wood to fuel the fire and carrying loads of cold water to replenish the condenser pot placed over the bubbling mash. This heated condenser water is used again for washing dishes and for feeding the water buffalo, who shakes its head vigorously if given cold water to drink. Gurung women don't drink alcohol, except to remedy frequent medical complaints, so Aama keeps most of the distilled *raksi* for relatives and guests, and sells the rest. Her house is directly below the path that leads to the neighboring Brahmin village just over the ridge, and is convenient for the high-caste teetotalers who drop off the trail on cold nights for a clandestine drink.

The Gurung's compulsive resourcefulness is almost an embarrassment to the casual observer. Axes, plows and digging tools are used until they are worn beyond recognition. The village blacksmiths then reincarnate the stubs into another generation of tools and utensils; Aama can recall the lineage of successive incarnations of each of her pots, ladles and hoes. Paper is folded and saved for wrapping spices, and corncobs reappear as everything from bottle stoppers to livestock feed. The chaff winnowed from millet is fed to livestock or used to stuff pillows.

Aama finds it hard to rest when there is work to be done, which is most of the time. She sleeps from four to six hours a night, working long after dark or rising well before sunrise, depending on whether the moon is waxing or waning. She believes that too much sleep will cause one to be drowsy during the waking hours, and that sleep during the day is an extravagant waste of useful time.

Aama will acknowledge sickness by carrying smaller loads, and she gauges the degree of her illness by the size of load she can carry. Even when sick she has to eat, she says, so chores come before convalescence. If very sick, Aama may ask those who come for a drink of alcohol to split firewood in lieu of money payment. Subtle discrimination among the villagers against old people also contributes to Aama's ardent dedication to work. Her son-in-law loans her his oxen only at the end of the plowing season, and some villagers make her feel obliged to treat them to a meal or a glass of spirits as if she were a wealthy widow on pension. She hopes that death will come quickly when she is no longer able to support herself. Even in her good health she is noticeably self-deprecating, ashamed of her dependency on Maaita and others to perform the heavier tasks that she used to manage alone.

Religion is an important and daily part of Aama's life. In the eyes of Hindus, the Gurung are considered to be spiritually inferior to the high-caste Brahmins of the lower valleys, but Hindu gods and legendary figures comprise only a part of the Gurung's pantheon. Their deities are molded from a unique combination of Hinduism, Buddhism, a form of Bön-po shamanism originating in pre-Buddhist Tibet, superstition, and local protective and wrathful spirits. Rather than being dogmatically exclusive, their varied religious beliefs and practices seem to be expanding to absorb more recent Western ideas as well. To Aama, these are all effectively the same *dharma*, or path, and few among the lay villagers distinguish between the unique historical origins and specific ritual details of their spiritual pathway.

In difficult situations, especially when she feels wronged or taken advantage of, Aama defers to the counsel of the dharma. She is sensitive to a growing wave of religious hypocrisy, and remains faithful to the dharma in spite of her temptation to speak and act impulsively. She is careful to conceal harsh feelings toward those who have lied or treated her disrespectfully—feelings which sometimes surface bitterly in the presence of close relatives or non-Gurungs, to whom she can speak without fear of reprisal. Similar to many, Aama finds it painful to reconcile her emotions with cultural and religious dictates.

Aama's integration into Gurung culture allows her to leave much unspoken. Her premonitions of future events, such as the arrival of a guest or sudden illness of a distant relative, are startlingly accurate. If she doubts the validity of her telepathic impressions, she calls a shaman to verify them. Some of these shamans routinely become entranced and are reported to travel in the underworld, a vaguely defined zone where evil spirits abound. During the trance, these spirits can become dramatically possessed in the body of the shaman. Many of these shamans have learned their reported ability to perceive and use supernatural powers from years of strict discipline under the guidance of a guru or close relative. Other untrained shamans, known as "sprung from the earth," can spontaneously tap these same forces. This capacity is usually recognized in their youth when, suddenly and disarmingly, the spirits manifest themselves in their bodies. The possessed villager may be performing a routine task, when he begins to shake, as if suffering an epileptic attack. The vision and curing ability of these amateur shamans is thought by many to be more profound than that of the trained shamans, though each individual is judged by the veracity of his predictions and effectiveness of his cures.

One of Aama's nephews has cured her illnesses several times by "blowing out" the spirits that infected her. Against Sun Maya's pleadings, she has more than once tried to refuse his treatment. She feels that her nephew will be too bothered to visit, and at her age fate should be the one to determine her future.

"OOOOOOOOHH...SAAIBOL...," bellows the town crier, calling the villagers to bring one rupee and one *mana* (1.5 pint) of uncooked rice to the meeting area below the main trail. These offerings are for payment to three lamas who have arrived after nearly three days' walk, contracted to perform a ritual to protect Danda against hail. Aama looks for her mana measuring cup, and remembers that her cousin in the house below has borrowed it. She instead fills a brass plate with rice, plants a rupee note on top and sends Maaita off to deliver it, telling her to have the town councilmen re-measure the rice with their cup, and to not forget to bring back the plate and excess rice.

Typical of most of the Gurung's rituals, the annual hail-protection ceremony lasts all night, the time when the spirits are most active. Danda villagers gather at the trail juncture where these spirits travel, and become absorbed in the rhythmic stomach-vibrating pulse of the lama's drums and conch shell blasts. Children play tag while the unmarried adolescents maintain a supercilious indifference to the ceremony, preferring to take advantage of the darkness for socializing and exploratory closeness. The lamas are nearly entranced, but spirit possession is not their intention at this time; underworld travel or interpretation of unforeseen recent events are not included in this ritual. They must attract

and capture the hail-causing spirits in a clay pot that has
been inverted over a small copper vessel filled with water,
and then systematically rid the village of them for the year.
These hail spirits are also drawn into plowshares, symbols
of the crop productivity which they have the power to reverse in minutes. Most households have brought their worn
plows to the ritual site to further attract the spirits. Aama
has slipped away to grind corn, but she is drawn back when
the chanting and drumming climax in the early morning
before sunrise, when the lamas conclude the service. They
remove the clay pot and examine the water vessel for the
change in clarity that represents the presence of the hail
spirits. Were there no color change, the ceremony would be
repeated. Finding that the spirits have entered, the lamas
escort the clay pot and vessel to a barren patch of land at the
edge of Danda. They bury it there with the worn plows, and
all return to their village and fields for another day's work.

Aama is inextricably bound to the life of Danda and the
surrounding Gurung villages by family ties and mutually
shared beliefs. Children and relatives are at the heart of her
identity, and her health and wealth are tied to that of the
extended family. Kinship terms, rather than names, are used
for address, constantly reinforcing the familial bond even
with distant relatives. A villager may have a dozen titles
depending on who is speaking to him. Aama's youngest
nephew addresses her by the kinship term *phaane*, meaning
"father's eldest sister," while the same nephew's wife addresses Aama as *phojo*. These kinship names also connote a
specific interrelationship, whether patronizing, respectful,
friendly, distrustful or available for marriage.

The extended family is a complicated and finely tuned
organism, though it can be precariously balanced. Relatives
are counted on in times of hardship to share a generosity
which is expected reciprocally. If a buffalo fails to calve or a
corn crop is destroyed by hail, close relatives will set aside

some of their yield for the affected one, whereas their own harvest may not have produced even a year's supply for themselves. Wealth is never a private affair. Those who have the means are generally obliged to give loans to those who don't. The debtor in turn will seldom offer to pay the loan until it is publicly apparent that he has generated the means to do so; the creditor will not ask until that time, unless he falls into financial difficulty. A mutual, subjective assessment of need usually determines the terms of a loan.

Outside the extended family, however, hostilities often build and simmer, usually over unfaithfulness, hoarding, or procrastination in the settlement of debts. Gossip replaces legal restraint in the enforcement of cultural taboos, and in the absence of personal privacy the sweeping influence of gossip is effective in controlling village behavior. An extra-marital affair will inevitably lead to expulsion of the couple from the village unless a stiff fine is paid to the jilted spouse. Every villager's income, debts, habits and desires are known to all. The young, in an attempt to reserve a degree of privacy at least within their peer group, have coined numerous neologisms, and in some villages even an entire jargon that is impenetrable by the village elders. When private confidences need sharing, Aama too will sometimes converse with those her own age using terms invented in their youth.

Wrist watches, water buffalos and real estate dominate the men's conversation in Danda. They trade and speculate on these commodities with the zeal of stock marketeers and the subtle legerdemain of seasoned poker players.

In Nepal it is now illegal to openly accuse anyone of being a witch. The stigma of such an accusation would be far too great for any village woman to bear, and there would be nowhere she could hide. Aama thinks there are currently no witches in Danda, but that there were previously. She suspects that the daughter of one of those now haunts the village of her birth.

The witch spirits are usually thought to infect a woman without her awareness, but some varieties are believed to have learned the craft from their mothers. A witch normally becomes active only at night, but she can covertly cast a spell or hex on people during the day as well. Gurung men occasionally join in nighttime witch hunts. Groups wielding sticks and curved *khukri* knives spread out in the fields near the sighting and attempt to corner the elusive form, blocking the paths which lead to the forest and the ceremony site on the ridge, a nocturnal witch haven. When they return to the village from an unsuccessful witch hunt, they can always claim that the witch escaped to the crematory ground; no one would consider going there to verify it. Talk about a woman suspected of practicing witchcraft, is hushed and guarded. In the company of such a woman the villagers are careful not to offend her for fear of the consequences.

Unlike witches, however, deer, leopards and blue sheep are no longer seen in the Gurung's hills, while jackals, martens and vultures now proliferate, overturning beehives and terrorizing chickens. Other than the dramatic weather patterns that visit Danda, some of the last vestiges of untamed nature are the horizon-spanning, V-formations of bar-headed geese which annually pass thousands of feet above the village, gaining altitude to cross the Himalayas to summer on the Tibet plateau. Called *kraank-ku-la* for their throaty honk, the geese possess a mystique with adults and children alike. They no longer stop at the ridgetop watering hole as they used to years ago, and few Gurung have seen one at close range, or out of formation. Around Danda, wildlife will probably never again reach its previous numbers.

Danda is in the center of Nepal's most densely populated hill district; there are now nearly three houses for every one of Aama's youth. Population is continuing to grow, agri-

cultural productivity is being lost through deforestation and
soil erosion, and Western values are undermining many of
their strongest traditions. Aama and her tribespeople's relaxed subsistence is quietly turning into a desperate struggle.
Emigration to the southern borderlands and an attempt to
start life over has been the only alternative for some. Those
who remain in the village are obliged to cultivate more
marginal lands and encroach further on the receding forests.
Hopefully, Aama's comparison of humans to trees that
grow, bloom, die and give birth to others in their place, is
not misconceived. In Nepal, young trees—and Aama's like
Vishnu Maya—are endangered and face an uncertain future.

This photograph was taken in a photo studio near Calcutta in 1952. Lal Prasad Gurung, Aama's husband, is in the left rear. Their daughter Sun Maya is in the front center. A friend of Sun Maya, with whom she has formed a bond of fictive kinship, is on the left.

Aama's nephew, with two male dancers from his barracks in the
British Gurka Army.